P9-DDX-331

MODELS, MENTORS, and MESSAGES
blueprints of urban ministry
Dr. René Rochester

ZONDERVAN®

ZONDERVAN.com/
AUTHORTRACKER
follow your favorite authors

youth
specialties

youth specialties

Models, Mentors, and Messages: Blueprints of Urban Ministry
Copyright 2009 by René Rochester

Youth Specialties resources, 300 S. Pierce St., El Cajon, CA 92020 are published by Zondervan, 5300 Patterson Ave. SE, Grand Rapids, MI 49530.

ISBN 978-0-310-28467-3

Cover design by David Conn
Interior design by Brandi Etheredge Design

Printed in the United States of America

09 10 11 12 13 14 • 20 19 18 17 16 15 14 13 12 11 10 9 8 7 6 5 4 3 2 1

ACKNOWLEDGMENTS

As I sit here at my kitchen table reflecting on all that's recently transpired in this nation, all I can say is, "To God be the glory, great things he has done!" When I was offered a contract to write this book, I never imagined that a few months prior to its release I would stand in my mother's living room and witness the first African American elected President of the United States. I stepped away for a moment to get my camera so I could capture my mother, sister, and nephew on film the moment the announcement occurred. Aaron Bates, an eight-year-old boy being raised by his mother and grandmother, now has a picture in his mind of another man of color raised in similar ways who is to become the 44th President of the United States.

For many President-elect Obama is a model who speaks of mentors and delivers a powerful message. But throughout the pages of this book I discuss the greatest role model this world has ever known: The Lord Jesus Christ. In these pages I share how Jesus used certain individuals in my life—those whom I lived among, listened to, and learned from—in order that I'd someday model, mentor, and speak messages of challenge, encouragement, and hope.

I would like to thank a few people who've helped me push out this book: My father, the late Frederick Douglas Rochester, for his musical genius and persistence and poise—a man who I've grown to know better through stories of his life I've heard others tell. My mother, Bernice R. Bates, who persevered and to this day continues to pray for me and believe in what God has deposited in me. Dr. Fred Peterson, who has witnessed my journey for 30 or so years, first as a wild sophomore at the University of Texas at Austin, and then welcoming me into a master's program in the early 1990s that was extremely difficult to enter, and then serving on my dissertation committee, cheering me on. Aunt Catherine, Uncle Clarence, and Uncle John for listening and sharing your stories. Marvin, Kawanda, Tommy, and Russ—for your prayers and encouragement when doubters and the enemy of discouragement was in full force. My Brentwood Academy colleague Jeff Bryant—you have been a constant voice of encouragement; thanks for welcoming my creativity! Dave Urbanski, you were great! You were patient and willing to push me through; Roni, your grace extended to me was a blessing; Jay, thanks for taking a chance! My friend Dr. Annita—thanks for traveling, teaching, reading, and researching with me. Your willingness to stand with me is a testimony of what I believe we should be modeling to the nation. Two sisters in Christ raised in two different worlds but called together by the Father for such a time as this! I love and appreciate you and am ready to cheer you on when you write your first book.

Finally to all who're positioned to model for and mentor this next generation—run your race with endurance and the encouragement of the empowering Holy Spirit!

—Dr. René Rochester, November 2008

CONTENTS

INTRODUCTION

The year was 1959. In a community hospital on Commonwealth Avenue in Boston, René Darlene Rochester was born to her proud parents, Frederick Douglas Rochester and Bernice Bryant Rochester.

Both of my parents were hard workers. My mother was a nurse at Children's Hospital in Boston. My father, a graduate of the New England Conservatory of Music, was an accomplished musician and a part-time instructor in voice and piano in the Fine Arts departments at both Boston University and Northeastern University. To support his family, he also worked evenings, playing dinner music at Hugo's Lighthouse Restaurant (now known as Atlantica) in Cohasset, Massachusetts.

My birth certificate looks like those of other children born that same year in our community: It contains the handwritten word *colored* in the space provided for race. I was born approximately five years after the historic *Brown v. Board of Education* ruling. On May 17, 1954, the U.S. Supreme Court ruled unanimously that racial segregation in public schools violated the Fourteenth Amendment to the Constitution. This ruling was then applied to other public facilities, and in the years following, other decisions struck down similar Jim Crow legislation.

I can only imagine the thoughts going through my parents' minds. Their two daughters (my sister, Karen, was born in 1956) would attend school alongside white students in the infancy of integration. This was a new day!

Well, nine months after my birth, things changed in the Rochester house. My father suffered a blood clot to his heart and died, and my mother was suddenly left to raise two daughters under the age of five on a single income. The financial and emotional pressures increased, and we had to move from Roxbury to the Jamaica Plain housing projects. We were, as the mothers of the church would say, "in the need of prayer."

So, what would be "the working model" or strategy of service to minister to my family? If you relied on the demographics of what you heard in your social work class or the "Ministering and Reaching the City" course, you might believe the wrong thing. For example: *"Baby mamma drama"—where's the father? Is he in prison or just shackin' so the mother can collect welfare checks?* But that wasn't the case in my family.

To better understand how to minister to my family, you would've needed to understand the ramifications of Jim Crow legislation and how it's impacted people living in many urban communities of America. The book of 1 Chronicles refers to this as *understanding the times* (1 Chronicles 12:32).

You'd also have to understand our culture. Understanding a culture comes from observing the people of a community. The ways people think, the languages they speak, the religious customs they follow, the foods they eat, their senses of humor, and their child-rearing styles and philosophies—these are just a few of the expressions that encompass a culture.

In my case, you would have discovered that the history of and conditions involved in my family's move to the projects had a pro-

found influence on my formative years, and God has used those experiences to prepare me for one of the many ministries to which I've
been called—training urban youth workers.

URBAN YOUTH MINISTRY MISCONCEPTIONS

Over the nearly two decades of my calling, I've seen and heard many
misconceptions about urban ministry and problems surrounding it.
For some, their ideas and methods are based on courses they took
in college. After finishing their bachelor's degrees, some of these individuals have left everything to work as missionaries within a particular inner city for a year, and now they're ready to give their lives
for the cause. Certain individuals feel that five years of relocation
to an urban community prepare them to be seasoned experts fully
equipped for any method of ministry.

Others may be involved in urban ministry because they were
moved by a speech they heard at a fundraising banquet.

Then there are those already living in urban communities who
have a heart for young people in the neighborhood, but they've been
so burned by the drive of past ministry agendas that they share things
like, "You can't tell *me*—I live here!"

And pastors of small churches may end up with staff members
handling a variety of youth issues and are genuine in their passion,
but they lack the skills or resources to effectively reach this fast-
paced generation.

Whatever the scenario, the answer begins with H.O.W.: **H**earing
God's voice, **O**beying God's voice, and **W**atching God work in you and
through you—wherever God places you. I believe God has called, appointed, and anointed individuals to serve youth in urban communities. The people of the city are waiting for these individuals to come

and live out the good news of the kingdom of God in their neighbor-hoods. I believe the urban minister (servant) must be one who has recognized the call of God, responded with a heart of repentance, and is willing to be reformed for his or her position and assignment.

BEGINNING THE PROCESS

One of the developmental tasks of childhood, the teenage years, and young adulthood is discovering and affirming one's identity. But what defines it? Is it a person's family ties, religious or spiritual experiences, sense of vocation, personal creed, or dreams and ideals?

When discussing big questions like this, the church often turns to its greatest—and always reliable—example: Jesus. And it's no different for this question. Indeed, one of the important things you'll discover in these pages is that Jesus affirmed his identity through his relation-ship with God in the midst of a community of people modeling God's kingdom culture.

Models, Mentors, and Messages: Blueprints of Urban Ministry gives you the opportunity to learn from Jesus—the Master Teacher—how to position yourself to be a co-laborer with God in serving the people of urban communities. For Jesus was called of God to fulfill a purpose on earth—just as you are. And he was the master of minister-ing to cities and villages—and you can be, too.

In chapter one we'll observe "the call of God" on Jesus' life and how we, too, must respond to the call. In chapters two through four, we'll observe the developmental stages of Jesus' life, focusing on how his family, his heavenly Father, his Jewish community, and neighbor-ing nations were all used to shape his destiny. You'll also read about how your own genetic propensities, your divine nature as a believer, and your call as a follower of Christ are what set in motion and ulti-mately influence your purposed destiny.

Jesus lived out the Word to those around him. In the days of his adult ministry, he continued to uphold his Jewish culture using parables and illustrations that pointed people to the concept of the One True God. In chapters five through nine, we'll see how Jesus' formative years growing up around other people groups prepared him to minister to the nations and train the Twelve to reach the world beyond Jerusalem.

In these pages you'll also learn about Jewish culture in Jesus' day. Judaism was more than a belief system. Certainly it encompassed religious laws—but it also involved sacred rituals and age-old customs; thousands of years of uninterrupted history; a spiritual, physical, and political attachment to the homeland of Israel; a commitment to social justice and righteousness; a deep love for learning; a dedication to the perpetuation of the Hebrew language; and varied cultural expressions in art, music, dance, and theater. To the Jewish people, everything they learned had a spiritual aspect to it. They lived and learned from a holistic mindset that everything was connected to the hand of Yehovah God. We'll also observe how the Greek Hellenistic culture began to compartmentalize learning.

Jesus handled God's claims while living in an earthly form. He dealt with the tension and inner conflict over human desires for social acceptance, loyalty to family, economic prosperity, and other ideals that we all struggle with. The writer of Hebrews tells us that Jesus triumphantly made decisions that allow us to have a High Priest who can sympathize with our challenges and weakness. We're also told that it wasn't easy for Jesus.

During the days of Jesus' life on earth, he offered up prayers and petitions with fervent cries and tears to the one who could save him from death, and he was heard because of his reverent submission. Son though he was, he learned obedience from what he suffered and, once made perfect, he became the source of eternal salvation for all

11

who obey him and was designated by God to be high priest in the order of Melchizedek. (Hebrews 5:7-10)

While on earth Jesus conquered the challenges of choosing to walk in obedience to his Father and fulfilling his call—even to his own death. Jesus' resurrection and empty grave prove him to be the ultimate role model and mentor.

Our Savior was born in human flesh, yet he had a divine Spirit. He was initially trained by models in both his family and in the Jewish community; but as Jesus came of age, he had to learn to submit not only to his earthly father—whom he could see—but also to his heavenly Father, the invisible God. His outer ear heard the voices of his family members and community, but his inner ear heard the voice of his heavenly Father.

I'm encouraged to know that Christ Jesus sent the Holy Spirit to lead us and guide us into all truth, enabling us with the power to obey. Throughout the pages of this book, you'll discover and learn to discern the voice of God among your family and community in order to make life decisions. This type of discernment is necessary for each of us to accomplish what we've been put here on earth to do. (And I hope you'll dig into the Questions for Discussion at the end of each chapter in small groups to further flesh things out.)

A UNIQUE ANGLE

Models, Mentors, and Messages is coming at you from a unique angle. Here you'll read about issues surrounding urban youth ministry from an exegetical *and* theological *and* experiential point of view—to say nothing of the fact that as a woman of color, practitioner, and academician, I've lived it and worked it and learned it. You'll read about issues that people tend to dance around, too. And despite all that's gone into the creation of this book (including the research), I don't think we can begin to talk about change in urban youth ministry without talking about the Holy Spirit—so I do that a lot in these pages, too. My aim has been to bring everything together that life has shown me and present something fresh and holistic that urban youth workers can use effectively.

IF YOU'RE ABOUT URBAN YOUTH MINISTRY, THIS BOOK IS FOR YOU

This book is for *whosoever* wants to do youth ministry in the urban venue. It doesn't matter what you are: Asian, African American, Caucasian, Latino, or another color or ethnicity or combination thereof; it doesn't matter if you're from the suburbs and feel led to serve in the inner city, or you're a native of the 'hood and need resources to better serve youth and their families—it's my prayer that this book will give you a better understanding of how to posture yourself to recognize the guidance of God in the urban landscape.

But beyond that, whoever you are and wherever you're headed, *you must learn about your community* and *learn from the people in your community.* Because issues specific to the culture you're trying to reach will come up. Are you willing to approach your mission with humility? If so, you've taken an important first step. For the remainder of your steps, my desire is that this book will help you learn more about effective, collaborative partnership and the cost of being willing to walk in community.

May we all be willing to pay the price and then receive the blessing of one day hearing: "Well done, good and faithful servant! Enter now into what I have prepared for you!"

CHAPTER ONE

SONSHIP AND DAUGHTERHOOD
THE HUMAN MODEL

But when the fullness of the time came, God
sent forth His Son, born of a woman,
born under the Law, so that He might redeem
those who were under the Law,
that we might receive the adoption as sons.
(Galatians 4:4-5, NASB)

Abraham Heschel, in his article on "The Spirit of Jewish Education," writes that what's needed most isn't textbooks but "text-people"—because the teacher's personality is the "text" that pupils will read and never forget.

We who are called to urban youth ministry must realize the power of being living *models* who dare to *mentor* and live out the *message* of the gospel. Jesus was sent on assignment by his Father to *model* on earth the *message* of a heavenly kingdom, and he *mentored* others to do likewise. Jesus is our blueprint. He displays the basic design for all ministries, whether they're rural, suburban, or urban.

Paul wrote to the church at Rome, "For everything that was written in the past was written to teach us, so that through the endurance taught in the Scriptures and the encouragement they provide we might have hope" (Romans 15:4). It's good news to know that others have already prepared a road for future generations to travel—we can learn not only from our biblical spiritual ancestors, but also from elders in our communities.

15

MY EXPERIENCE IN EAST AUSTIN

I spent my early childhood years in Boston and most of my adult life in Austin, Texas. I was privileged to earn an athletic scholarship and become a member of the Lady Longhorn basketball and track teams at the University of Texas at Austin (UT). That's where I received my first lesson in urbanization and gentrification.

It all began during my recruiting trip. I received a tour of the city, and I saw how the university influenced the surrounding community. Everywhere we went, I saw the Longhorn emblem and school colors (burnt orange and white). But it wasn't until I was in need of a perm that I became aware of East Austin. It was a whole new world that didn't have the Longhorn insignia.

The year was 1977, and UT had six African-American students in the women's athletic program—five of us on the track team, and two of us on the basketball team. (I was on both teams.) We ate together and rode in the same van on trips. And the older students of color let the freshmen know where to go partying and get our hair done.

Minnie's Beauty Salon was just across the highway off East 12th Street. When I walked into the salon wearing my Longhorn sweat-shirt, I had no idea the boundaries I was crossing. During those first several minutes, not much was said; but everyone felt the instant climate change. When Minnie began working on my hair, she casually noted, "It's your sweatshirt." I asked a few questions, and she gave me a history lesson about East Austin and its relationship (or should I say, lack thereof) with the University of Texas.

I heard about Huston-Tillotson University (HTU), the historical-ly black college located around the corner from her shop, and how many of her clients were affiliated with the school. I listened intently and let her know that I, too, was from "the east side" in a sense, too—albeit of Brockton, which is south of Boston.

UT wasn't very popular in East Austin in those days. As the university continued to build, it expanded to the east and bought up land where generations of African-American families lived. Dr. Charles Urdy—a former professor at Huston-Tillotson University and former Austin City Council member—lived through the changes in East Austin:

"East 11th and East 12th Street were the heart and soul of East Austin. Practically everything we needed or wanted was either on those streets or near those streets. It was sort of the business hub for East Austin. And it is where most people spent most of their time outside of work. Most people only left East Austin to go to work."

This healthy, vibrant community actually disintegrated as integration happened. Opportunities drew young adults away from the East Austin community, and consequences included a decline in business, an increase in crime, a weakening of schools, and marginalization. Integration in Austin proper appeared beneficial, but not in East Austin. Despite an urban renewal effort started in the 1960s (and, many believe, never completed) and multiple infrastructure improvements, Austin has been unable to assist East Austin in its economic and social transition. (Cited from http://www.klru.org/austinnow/archives/gentrification/index.php)

So which models and mentors can assist communities experiencing this type of transitional change? Many of us know there's a need for change in our personal lives and communities, but we struggle with the process of transition.

LEVELING THE FIELD

The announcement at Jesus' purposed birth was "Joy to the world, the Lord is come! Let earth receive her King." At the time of Jesus' birth, world leaders didn't know what to do with a message like that. The colonized Jewish culture was still living under the oppression of a

Roman government, but they understood that when a new king was enthroned, there were new agendas to be accomplished. Jesus came to proclaim and establish heaven's kingdom agenda on earth.

We, like the colonized Jewish community in Jesus' day, often get stuck in or frustrated by the agendas of human systems when it comes to change and transition. East Austin, like many other cities, struggled through the transition of desegregation and industrialization. Problems evolved during that time, such as poverty, street crime, and gang-related activities. I believe these problems persist because we tend to focus on the statistics, which are merely symptoms of deeper community problems. Is there a way to reach the *roots* of these problems?

Recently a friend and I were sitting at my kitchen table when we felt a rumble that shook the floor of the house. My friend nodded and said, "They're blasting to build new houses." This blasting procedure enables builders to dig deep because it removes the old rubble and rock that prevents the creation of level ground. In our communities today, there are some rocks and rubble that need removing. They're what I call *isms*—racism, capitalism, sexism, and denominationalism, just to name a few—and they can get in the way of building God's kingdom in the city. The good news is that the message of God's kingdom lets us know there is a leveling place.

God sent his Son Jesus to earth to proclaim and demonstrate that we all come from the same spiritual ancestry of Adam; and because Adam was unable to fulfill God's plan for his creation, *the man Christ Jesus* (1 Timothy 2:5) is the second Adam. Once you and I become children of God, we all inherit the same bloodline and kingdom privileges as Jesus—no matter our ethnicity, social status, or neighborhood. And it's on this level ground where we can begin to build a sure foundation (1 Corinthians 3:11).

Jesus said a wise person is like one who hears the Word of God and obeys it (Matthew 7:24-27). When this person digs deep and arrives upon the rock or level ground—Jesus Christ—only then can this person begin building a house that can withstand the storms of economic crisis, segregation, poverty, and whatever else may happen in the urban community. Similarly, when our foundations are built well, they cannot be destroyed.

MENTORS ON EARTH (AND A MENTOR IN HEAVEN)

In the beginning, God revealed himself in all the works of creation. Christ was with God and the Holy Spirit when they spread the heavens and laid the foundations of the earth. It was his hand that set the universe in place and fashioned the flowers of the field. The psalmist tells us in Psalm 65 that the God of our salvation is "the hope of all the ends of the earth and of the farthest seas" (v. 5). Then he goes on to say, "who formed the mountains by your power" (v. 6). But I love the part that says he "stilled the roaring of the seas, the roaring of their waves, and the turmoil of the nations" (v. 7).

Mark 4:35-41 records how Jesus woke up and revealed himself as God while the disciples panicked. God who created the heavens and earth was now in human form (Jesus Christ), and he spoke to the wind, rain, and waves and calmed the sea.

We all go through life drama from time to time, and it can seem as real as the storm-tossed boat that carried the disciples. When I was walking through my doctoral program, there were many difficult battles. I was the first African American in my program, and not everybody felt I belonged there. At times even I doubted my place.

One night I drove to San Antonio, Texas, to spend some time with my pastor, Dr. Claudette A. Copeland. She drove me around the city and let me cry, shout, and fuss. She patiently handed me tissue after tissue, and then after a while she said to me: "You will not drown!" Pastor C was confident in the One who'd already prayed for me and formed me in my mother's womb. Pastor C knew all too well the battle that goes on inside the mind, emotions, and body because she and her husband, Bishop David M. Copeland, were the first African-American chaplain couple in the Air Force, and she is also a cancer survivor. Out of our relationship I've developed a trust in her wisdom and sensitivity as she modeled and mentored me through stormy seasons in my life.

I believe the people who survive and thrive in urban ministry are individuals who are mentored by men and women seasoned in their faith. These people are convinced that the same God who made the sea and calmed it can certainly handle our situations. God filled the earth with beauty and the air with song. And upon all things in earth and sky, he wrote the message of the Father's love.

But even more, there is someone who holds the blueprint of urban ministry. He's modeled it and even mentored some young people so they could do the same. It's Jesus Christ! And the rest of this book will show you how he did it.

A CONVINCING BLUEPRINT

I submitted my life to the Lord Jesus Christ at the age of 20, and that's when learning about God became a desirable thing. I didn't know the Bible at all. In fact the night my journey with Christ began, I went to church, and the pastor asked the congregation to turn to the book of John. I had a small Gideon Bible, so I flipped to the *books* of John (the epistles). I said to myself, *1 John, 2 John, 3 John*. And then I asked the young lady sitting next to me, "Which one?"

She said, "There's another one," and she showed me the Gospel of John. A hunger to know the Bible and its Author began.

I was like the newborn baby Peter referred to—longing for the milk of the Word (1 Peter 2:2). I had a boatload of questions! One morning I read Jeremiah 33:3, "Call to me and I will answer you and tell you great and unsearchable things you do not know." That verse encouraged me to search God's Word for life's answers. And I had so many questions: *What about slavery? What should women's roles be in the church? Why is there poverty and injustice?* The list went on and on.

My understanding of the characteristics of a citizen of God's kingdom grew—and so did my passion to stand against injustice. However, my frustration was that I was still encountering sexism, racism, and other inequalities...but it was within the *Christian* community. Therefore, my questions changed from *Why are these things happening?* to *How then shall we live?*

Paul prayed that the believers at Colosse would be filled with the knowledge of Christ's will in all wisdom and spiritual understanding so they could walk in a manner worthy of God—fully pleasing him, being fruitful in every good work, and increasing in their knowledge of him (Colossians 1:9-10). We can learn much from this prayer.

Likewise, Jesus told his disciples, "If you've seen me, then you've seen the Father who sent me" (John 14:9, *my paraphrase*). In other words, Jesus' will is synonymous with God's will. "Thy kingdom come, Thy will be done in earth, as it is in heaven" (Matthew 6:10, KJV). God's kingdom fulfillment was the will of the Father, and it can be established only with a person's recognition and acknowledgment of God being ultimately in control. Yet this is where many of us get frustrated—when we feel as though things are out of control, or we're no longer in control.

Our progressive growth in the knowledge of God comes through life's experiences. God will use what we go through as personal points of reference. And I believe God releases an understanding of his Word in our lives according to our ability to handle what he shows us. At times we'll all experience storms (injustice, racism, and so on) that are greater than what our human resources can manage. The question is, *Are we able to model or point others to the Model—Christ Jesus—who knows God's strength and power?* It will take supernatural strength to endure these difficult times with joy.

TROUBLE ACROSS THE URBAN TERRAIN

Many urban venues have been living in residual social instability. The absence of community to motivate isolated individuals and poor families toward a sense of belonging and control is a big problem. However, I believe the body of Christ is the venue that can motivate these individuals and encourage the growth of shared values again in the urban community.

And if we're called to serve in these venues, then we must learn from the Master Teacher of urban ministry—Jesus Christ. He lived it, modeled it, and designed the blueprint of how to reach people everywhere. And he left us a message that proclaims hope. We must continue to ask for grace and strength to walk alongside individuals experiencing an awakening and empowerment given by the Spirit of God. Let's pray for change in their personal lives and community.

JESUS MODELED HANDS-ON MINISTRY

For years urban sociologists, and now *urban theologists* (or theologians), have discussed the concerns of the nature of the city. We can learn much from their studies, but we must be careful not to make an idol of the art of discussion. The apostle Paul challenged a group of believers in Corinth with these words: "Knowledge puffs up, but love edifies" (1 Corinthians 8:1, NKJV).

Jesus, God's replica on earth, did not confine himself to the ivory towers of his day, merely reasoning and discussing in the temple or synagogue about the problems in Jerusalem and the rest of the known world. He came proclaiming a new way of thinking about the community—and did so openly, before all people. Jesus was convinced of his message and mission, and he went forth preaching, "Repent, for the kingdom of heaven is at hand" (Matthew 4:17, NKJV).

In the same way, we must be able to *walk* in our knowledge—not just talk about it. If children in the community cannot read, we must teach them how. If the elderly in the community need assistance, we must serve them. If there are known drug lords and pimps controlling the community, we must pray for them and ask for God's wisdom for how we can get more involved in social action and help clean up the community. Because in my experience, the drug lords *know* the men and women of God in their neighborhoods. We don't need to command the pimps to leave "in Jesus' name." It doesn't even take confrontation—just presence. I've heard time and time again of dangerous individuals just packing up and moving out of their brothels and crack houses all because traffic to their places of business declined so sharply with the consistent presence of the Body of Christ there.

DO YOUR HOMEWORK

As a graduate student, I sat in classes and engaged in open dialogue about the disparities in health care, education, and juvenile risk-taking behavior between urban and non-urban communities. My professors encouraged discussion, but they also mandated that we do research to back up our comments and opinions before we shared them. If professors challenge their students to do their homework before they speak, then how much more should we become students of the Word of God to learn God's heart and plan for the people of the world? Living among, learning about, and loving the people of the city we're called to is exactly what Jesus did.

In 1903, German sociologist George Simmel noted (in a classic essay called "The Metropolis and Mental Life") that city dwellers are bombarded by a tremendous amount of nervous stimulation, such as noise, traffic, crowds, the rapid pace of life, and dozens of other stimuli. He concludes that people living in the city simply cannot pay attention to everything that goes on around them; and as a result, they can become indifferent to their surroundings. Simmel's perspective is that since urbanites in particular deal with many strangers, their relationships with others tend to be directed toward goals rather than personal satisfaction.

Louis Wirth's famous essay "Urbanism as a Way of Life" reaches similar conclusions. Wirth believed that urban dwellers know one another only in superficial and impersonal ways. One person is recognized as a banker, another as a coworker, and still another as a cab driver; but the interpersonal depth seldom gets more intimate than that.

High-Tech, Low-Touch

More than a century later, things have escalated. Young people today—whether urban dwellers or not—are constantly impacted by blogs, MySpace, Facebook, Twittering, instant messaging, and texting. I teach high school, and I know just as you do that these technological modes of communication help create fragmented, shallow relationships. We all know teenagers are apt to text rather than converse with their vocal chords; but they're also texting five people at once—and some of them are in the same room! No intimacy, no social development—and very few are ever known by anybody. Alone in a crowd. But what happens when life goes downhill? When teenagers have to deal with difficulties? How do they lean on a shoulder when there's no shoulder around? Who are their good friends? Yes, we're high-tech...but we're also low-touch. And worse, when kids get their feelings hurt with no one to talk to, the pain and frustration build up—and instead of a fistfight or shouting match, out come the guns.

You see, technology (especially the gaming subculture) has trained young people to react rather than process—so much so that the emotional center of the brain is bypassed to such a regular extent that it's a habitual process, no matter if they're gaming or texting at the time or not. That's why it can be very difficult for teens to hold a conversation. I know some athletes who are in their early 30s chronologically, but they're 15 socially—and it's all due to learned behavior. No social skills, no emotional processes happening.

ONE RESPONSE: HOLISTIC MINISTRY

In any ministry dealing with young people—not just in urban settings—we need to more effectively recognize the needs of the whole person. Take a family living in a poor housing community—can their situation change? Can the parents and children be encouraged or changed from the inside out? It's not about just caring for the spiritual—especially when immediate physical needs aren't being met. Don't worry: God is big enough to handle all the problems in anybody's life, no matter how deep or how numerous.

ANOTHER RESPONSE: DEALING WITH SPIRITUAL OPPRESSION

Oppression is a word I heard often as I was growing up. But it wasn't until I began growing in my walk with Christ and reading the Bible that I got a kingdom definition of the word.

The first 10 years of my childhood were in the midst of the civil rights movement. I was four years old when President John F. Kennedy was assassinated, and I was eight when Dr. Martin Luther King's life was snuffed out. I witnessed firsthand the exchange of cruelty between people groups. That's when I first heard the word *oppression* in a sentence.

The Scriptures use the word *oppressed* to show one person or people group positioning themselves as superior to another and then purposely doing things to keep others subordinate to them. But Acts 10:38 tells us that people were also oppressed by the Devil. This form of *oppression* speaks of the superiority and manipulation that Lucifer used before God dismissed him from heaven. Indeed, the very characteristics of oppression originated with the self-seeking being we now call Satan.

Lucifer desired to be first in heaven. He attempted to gain control of, to manipulate, the other heavenly beings in order to draw them away from their Creator and win their worship for himself. Lucifer's desire for self-exaltation and his other evil characteristics enabled him to deceive a portion of the angels. But this led to his being hurled to the earth where he's been deceiving human beings ever since. Lucifer, now called Satan, leads us to doubt the Word of God and to distrust God's goodness. Satan also causes us to view God as harsh and unforgiving. And after all of these years, Satan's plan hasn't changed: It's to lure people in rebellion against God. That's why humans need a Redeemer, someone to get us back to God's original intent.

OUR MODEL OF A DIVINE NATURE

Adam originated with a divine nature, and the second Adam did as well. Christ was born of God (divine seed) and of a woman (human birth). He came into the world like all of us did—from his mother's womb. But prior to Christ's entrance in a manger, he was a citizen of heaven.

You and I, on the other hand, were born into the world as citizens of the earth. But once we're born again of the Spirit of God (John 3:3), we become citizens of heaven. And as children of God, we're commissioned to carry out the mandate of the government of heaven. Jesus proclaimed: "Thy kingdom come, Thy will be done in earth, as it is in heaven" (Matthew 6:10, KJV).

To be born of God is a powerful thought. The biblical term that's translated into English as *born of* is the same word used throughout the genealogies in the New Testament. It's the same word that's used when the angel tells Mary she'll "be with child" and give birth to a Son (Luke 1:31). I can understand Mary's confusion. She hadn't had sexual relations with a man, yet she was told she'd soon be pregnant.

The angel said to Mary:

"The Holy Spirit will come upon you, and the power of the Most High will overshadow you; and for that reason the holy Child shall be called the Son of God. And behold, even your relative Elizabeth has also conceived a son in her old age; and she who was called barren is now in her sixth month. For nothing will be impossible with God." (Luke 1:35-37, NASB)

We know that Elizabeth did conceive in her old age—a miraculous pregnancy and birth. And Mary was able to relate to her cousin Elizabeth, her human model, because Mary had experienced her own miracle as well.

KINGDOM GENETICS

Genetics is known as the natural innate endowment of all our characteristics, such as eye and hair color, personality, and immunities. The blood in our veins carries traces of DNA, and it's through the bloodline that we find our genetic lineage. People living in the Jewish culture in which Jesus was raised believed they were beneficiaries of the blessings of Abraham's ancestral line, and therefore, sons of God.

But in the book of John, Jesus says the only way we can become children of God is through spiritual regeneration (John 3:5). Being born of God means that no human has anything to do with it; this new birth comes through the will of God—through God's own unlimited power and unfailing love.

This, as noted previously, is the leveling place for all human beings. No matter the race, creed, culture, community dwelling, or social strata, all who are created in the image of God and have acknowledged his Son as our Lord and Savior become one—even as Jesus and his Father are one!

The rest of the book will discuss how Jesus of Nazareth (God come in the flesh) was raised with a heavenly heritage and earthly traditions that shaped him for his destiny. His life journey can teach us how he modeled a kingdom culture, mentored the disciples through it, and left us with a Helper (the Holy Spirit) to enable us to be a living epistle of the kingdom message.

DR. RENÉ'S PRESCRIPTION
for Vibrant Sonship and Daughterhood

- Level the field
- Seek mentors seasoned in their faith
- Prepare for storms
- Serve
- Do your homework
- Strive for holistic ministry
- Confront spiritual oppression

QUESTIONS FOR DISCUSSION

1. We as living models have the opportunity to function as mentors who live out the message of Christ. *How would you describe Jesus' life as a blueprint for modeling the message of gospel in the urban youth ministry landscape?*

2. Communities are cultures of interactive people groups in relationships. I share in this chapter my experiences in East Austin and that community's history in relation to the University of Texas. *What have you witnessed and experienced in a community that was closed to multicultural interactions because of past painful relationships? How can these barriers be addressed positively?*

3. How are old "isms" (sexism, racism, ageism, etc.) impacting the city you live in and work in?

4. Paul discussed some Jewish traditions that were abused in such a way that it hindered new believers from understanding their freedom and identity in Christ (e.g., circumcision, special foods—read Colossians 2:8, 20-23). *How have we built traditional truths into today's gospel message that God might want to break up and replace with freedom to experience Christ?*

5. Harnessing our positions as models in our communities (or as stated by Abraham Heschel, becoming "text people") is one way we can effectively stay on course through storms and confusing times of our journey. Read 2 Corinthians 3:2-6 and 4:1. *How are storms used to discourage and derail individuals in the ministries to which they've been called? What are some things you can do to avoid being derailed and discouraged?*

6. What are some ways that you as a leader can recognize redemptive potential and possibilities of at-risk youth and help them develop and grow in that potential?

CHAPTER TWO

FAMILY MODELS
PROVIDING THE FIRST MODELS, MENTORS, AND MESSAGES

Several years ago I was in Philadelphia serving as a guest speaker at a conference. During the closing session, a young man sang an old gospel hymn in a classical style. I couldn't help but notice his piano accompanist: An elderly man who played with such poise. Being in my father's hometown, I wondered if the pianist knew my father. Walking along the outside wall of the convention hall, I slowly made my way to the front to try to catch the gentleman as he left the stage.

When I finally reached his side, I stopped the man and said, "Excuse me, sir. Does the name Frederick Rochester mean anything to you?"

He paused for a moment and said, "Yes, a brilliant musician."

I didn't get to ask him anything else because he was being ushered out the door. But I went back into the ballroom and waited for an opportunity to speak to the young vocalist. When I did, I told him that I'd been a speaker at the beginning of the conference and that Philadelphia is my father's hometown. I asked him if he knew anyone who could tell me something about my father. He took my pen and wrote a name and phone number on the back of a manila envelope and said I should give this gentleman a call.

I couldn't get back to my hotel room quick enough. My heart was racing as I dialed the number, and then a man answered the phone.

I said, "Hello, sir. You don't know me. But my name is René Rochester, and I'm the daughter of Frederick Rochester, the pianist. I was wondering if you knew my father."

He replied, "Oh yes, I did know Fred. He would come by the church, and I'd open it up for him so he could practice the piano and play the organ. He was some kinda musician."

The gentleman couldn't see my face, but I was so proud to hear those words. I then asked a deeper question: "Do you know if my father was a Christian?"

He politely said, "Doesn't the Good Book tell us *you will know them by their fruit?* Your father was a man of character."

Later that evening I was leaving my Aunt Mary's house, and I put my briefcase on my shoulder as I walked to the car.

She said, "Mmm...the fruit don't fall far from the tree. You are Fred's child." She went on to say that I carried my briefcase like he did, and I walked like him, too. I thought to myself how amazing it is that you can act like someone you've never met. Some things we learn; others are a part of our genetic design.

A SEED IS PLANTED

Since the beginning of time, God ordained that every living creature would multiply after his or her own kind. Every tree yields a characteristic fruit along with its seed, and from that seed comes another tree that matures, continuing the cycle (Genesis 1:11-12). The interesting thing about a seed's growth is that it doesn't happen overnight. It takes time and cultivation.

God placed Adam in the garden and told him to cultivate the ground—that was his responsibility. He'd trim back the fast-growing plants to allow the healthy growth of everything God had created. Adam wasn't given the task to grow anything, but to keep the environment *conducive to growth.*

The Psalmist compares a wife who's borne children with her righteous husband to a fruit-bearing vine (Psalm 128). And a vinedresser who takes the time to tend to her vine is like a mother and father who take the time to train up their child. Mom, Dad, and those of us sharing in kinship care have a responsibility to keep a child's environment healthy and conducive to growth. (Again, we don't cause the growth—God does that; we just try to keep the paths straight.)

Growth and *development* are two terms often associated with education. There are numerous manifestations of growth and education, such as formal education, which comes through an institution designed for a specific group of learners (the local high school, a Sunday school class, and so on), or informal education, which a child receives when his mother or father teaches him while they're playing in the yard or working together in the kitchen. *Education* can even refer to what children learn from what's modeled in the neighborhood.

Webster's says *educate* means "to train by formal instruction or a supervised practice especially in a skill, trade, or profession; to develop mentally, morally, or aesthetically especially by instruction; to provide with information; to persuade or condition to feel, believe, or act in a desired way."

In all of these definitions, the focus is on the instructor. Our growth and development is all about the maturing process, and I believe it begins in the home or during the early years of our lives.

Education begins the day we're born. It starts with our mothers who carried us, and it progresses to others whom God has ordained to assist in our shaping.

Jesus is no exception.

Like any other mother, Mary carried her baby in her womb, went through labor, and then gave birth to a son—the Son of God. Then Mary and Joseph laid the foundation of Jesus' learning and mentoring by beginning his training in their home.

BY BLOOD OR BY EXTENSION, "WE ARE FAMILY"

In today's African-American culture, the term "Mamma 'n' them" describes the extended family and others who aren't actual blood relatives but who possibly live in the home and are treated as family. As a child, I spent time in Richmond, Virginia, in the summers. It was common in our family to find a cousin, niece, or nephew taken in by a grandmother, aunt, uncle, and even family friend. We were a community.

Andrew Billingsley, author of *Climbing Jacob's Ladder*, describes the African-American family as "an *intimate association* of persons of African descent who are *related to one another* by a variety of means, including blood, marriage, formal adoption, informal adoption, or by appropriation."

A CLOSER LOOK AT "FAMILY"

Definitions of family may vary based on the community or culture. Biblically there's evidence of a variety of family settings. During biblical times families were united by common blood or a common dwelling place. Noah's family included his wife, his sons, and their wives (Genesis 7:1,7). Jacob's family comprised three generations and included the servants, resident aliens, stateless persons, widows, and orphans who all lived under the protection of the head of the family (Genesis 46:8-26).

In my experience, there were certain house rules or protocol when living under the protection of someone's home. I recall kitchen discussions when a teenager disrespected an adult. The head of the house would say, "As long as you're under *my* roof and not paying any bills, this is how it will be. And if you can't abide by the rules of this house, then it's time to go!" Too often, we fail to realize the benefits of living under the protective covering of a home. It's a place to lay your head at night, and it provides regular meals. But one of the most important things established in a home are values.

As we journey through this chapter, we'll take a look at Jewish customs and the culture of childrearing and education. It's my prayer that the examples given will encourage those who desire to raise and train children and youth in a God-fearing manner.

Education, Now and Then

In Jesus' day the Jewish culture viewed education as the power to influence the next generation. Formal education did take place, but most education was informal (for example, how the people ate their meals, worked hard, made good friends, and sought advice before acting). The wise would educate the people living in their villages in terms of how to carry on successfully from one generation to the next. Most of what took place in their culture was designed so the next generation could witness the hand of God in all things. From the day a child was conceived, the parents knew they needed to depend on the God who allowed them to conceive to also develop and grow their child in the fullness of his or her God-ordained purpose.

In those days, everything was designed to point back to the Lord; but today that mindset is not so common. Life is compartmentalized—

especially with our overscheduled youth: There's a set time to be spiritual, to go to school, to participate in extracurriculars, for part-time jobs...and then there are family needs and peer relationships. So how do we minister to this compartmentalized, heavily programmed generation? First we have to do what we can to be integrated/holistic people ourselves—to not fall for compartmentalization ourselves. Then we go to them and teach them there's a whole new way of living—and outside the box.

Parents Have Needs, Too

Mary and Joseph were engaged, and then Joseph learned that Mary was pregnant. He knew he hadn't been intimate with her. Mary told him an angel spoke to her and told her she would conceive "of the Holy Spirit" and give birth to the Messiah.

> But the angel said to her, "Do not be afraid, Mary, you have found favor with God. You will conceive and give birth to a son, and you are to call him Jesus. He will be great and will be called the Son of the Most High. The Lord God will give him the throne of his father David, and he will reign over the house of Jacob forever; his kingdom will never end." (Luke 1:30-33)

> But after he had considered this, an angel of the Lord appeared to him in a dream and said, "Joseph son of David, do not be afraid to take Mary home as your wife, because what is conceived in her is from the Holy Spirit. She will give birth to a son, and you are to give him the name Jesus, because he will save his people from their sins." (Matthew 1:20-21)

Now let's picture a different scenario—Joe down the block. I can hear Joe say to Mary, "Hold up, now! I know I haven't been with you, so who's the baby's daddy?" Sometimes we fail to look at the reality of Jesus' humanity and the family he came from because we believe such information may keep others from believing in Jesus—or maybe we can't deal with it ourselves. But one of the reasons God sent his Son to be among us was so we can see how a *child of God* is supposed to live.

Can you imagine what went through both of their minds, knowing the Jewish custom of marriage and the laws of Moses regarding the infidelity of an engaged woman? The emotional strain was probably overwhelming. In their book *Dr. Spock's Baby and Child Care*, Benjamin Spock and Steven J. Parker talk about parents having needs, too. Spock points out that many books have been written about childcare, including theirs, but much of the emphasis has been placed on the child's needs. On the flip side, parents have emotional, social, spiritual, and psychological needs that must also be met in order for them to become healthy parents.

For years my mother struggled to be the best parent she could for her girls. I shared earlier how my father died when I was nine months old. At the time of his death, he was employed part time as the choirmaster and organist at a Methodist church not far from Boston University. He also held other jobs, such as working as an accompanist at Northeastern University where he composed and played for several productions. But because of segregation in the '50s, my father wasn't considered full-time staff. This made his passing even more difficult for my mother because without a full-time job, my father had no benefits.

Everything happened so quickly, and life had suddenly changed. My mother attended two funerals for my father—one in Boston and the other in Philadelphia (where my father was buried). In my mother's words, "I was young and emotionally distraught. I didn't know at the time what I was going to do. There was no money, and I had a three-year-old and a nine-month-old baby." But I recognize in my mother's story the hand of God meeting us. The Word tells us that God is "a father to the fatherless, a defender of widows" (Psalm 68:5).

her words, God will take care of them!

Someone told my mother about public welfare, so she got a sitter for me and took my older sister, Karen, with her to the welfare office. It was a frustrating day. The woman who was working with my mother assumed Mom was just trying to work the system, so she was extremely rude to her and even pushed Karen aside to get to her filing cabinet. Then the woman asked my mother in a sarcastic tone, "You *do* know where your husband is, don't you?" My mother had taken about all she could handle by this point, but she managed to tell the woman the name of the cemetery where my father is buried.

As the story goes, my mother, sister, and I were placed in the Jamaica Plain housing projects in Boston. Our years in the projects weren't easy, and there were all kinds of strains on my mother. But she was able to get part-time work as a licensed practical nurse. She did what she knew to do to get Karen and me through those early childhood years.

Mary and Joseph probably struggled through other times of being misunderstood as well. There were likely fears, doubts, and even physical and emotional exhaustion at times. But the good news is that the same God who delivered them can and will deliver urban youth and families today. Many times our most authentic models are individuals who've wrestled through life's challenges and learned to trust God in difficult situations. These people can be the source of internal faith and strength to encourage and empower the next generation with things they've personally experienced.

I have worked with in-school suspension monitors in a public school. The monitors all have degrees of some sort, but not teaching certificates—so they're living in an in-between place professionally, and some of them are discouraged. But I challenge them to use their present circumstances for good. It's the same thing if you work in urban youth ministry and are discouraged. You don't have to be a master scholar in youth development to minister and work with these kids—you just have to be available. If you love sports, use sports; the idea is to teach what you know. Authenticity comes from you being you. Wear your own shoes.

Growing in Faith and Authenticity

And what did Mary and Joseph learn while raising Jesus? First, that the needs of infants and children must be met by parents and others assigned to assist in their developmental process. There's an enormous amount of work that goes into childcare: Preparing the proper diet, washing clothes, changing diapers, cleaning up messes, drying tears, stopping fights, listening to the child's first attempts at language, and reading the same stories over and over again—just a few of the things parents have to walk through with their developing children.

But when the parent is a teenager, things are more complicated. Consider the emotional trauma in the life of an adolescent who's active in the church community, whose parents are probably known in the congregation—and then this young lady learns she's pregnant. Questions, fear, and confusion flood her thinking: *How am I going to raise a child? What is my family going to say? What will the people in the neighborhood and at church think?*

In the 2006 film *The Nativity Story*, the storyline follows two teenage parents who wrestled through these questions—and more—after the conception of Jesus. Once pregnant, Mary says, "How can this be...?" (Luke 1:34, NKJV). The angel Gabriel responds by assuring Mary that she is not alone and offering her a tangible place of connection. He tells Mary about her cousin Elizabeth who had a similar miraculous experience with the conception of John: "Consider your relative Elizabeth—even she has conceived a son in her old age, and this is the sixth month for her who was called barren. For nothing will be impossible with God" (Luke 1:36-37, HCSB). Notice how he encouraged Mary to hold on to the Word of the Lord: "For no word from God will ever fail" (Luke 1:37). Mary responds with confidence and faith: "Behold the maidservant of the Lord! Let it be to me according to your word" (Luke 1:38, NKJV).

First, Mary responded to the spiritual—"nothing will be impossible with God"—and she spoke words of faith showing her willingness to be used of God and her belief that God could and would do it. "I am the Lord's slave. May it be done to me according to your word" (Luke 1:38, HCSB). Scripture tells us that "without faith it is impossible to please God" (Hebrews 11:6) and that "faith comes from hearing the message, and the message is heard through the word about Christ" (Romans 10:17). And second, Mary put her faith into action by quickly heading out to visit Elizabeth.

So what had Mary and Elizabeth already learned that caused them to be able to embrace the words spoken by the angel? These women grew up in Jewish homes where it was part of the culture to tell the "stories of the Torah" (the writings of Moses). Therefore, these women were familiar with the first commandment in the Torah: "Be fruitful and multiply; fill the earth and subdue it" (Genesis 1:28, NKJV). They'd heard how God had caused other barren women to conceive—models such as Rachel, Hannah, and especially Sarah— the wife of the patriarch Abraham.

Both Elizabeth and Mary knew about Sarah. She'd overheard a conversation between the Lord and Abraham in which God said Sarah would have a child. (Elizabeth could really relate to the story of Sarah, as she was also beyond the age of childbearing when she conceived John.) Sarah laughed to herself because she was old and past the age of childbearing: "After I have become shriveled up and my lord is old, will I have delight?" (Genesis 18:11-12, HCSB). Yet Abraham chose to believe that God could do anything! He, like Mary and Elizabeth, chose to believe the angel's words.

Knowing Sarah's thoughts, the angel (God) continued to speak: "Why did Sarah laugh, saying, 'Can I really have a baby when I am old?' Is anything impossible for the Lord? At the appointed time I will come back to you, and in about a year she will have a son" (Genesis 18:13-14, HCSB).

Mary's life shows us the blessing of having someone we can relate to, to walk with us through difficult times. Today we have all kinds of support groups—for parents-to-be about to give birth... and for those having difficulty raising their child or teenager. We even have venues for youth workers to become more real and authentic with one another. Isn't it good to know that "Two are better than one, because they have a good return for their labor" (Ecclesiastes 4:9)?

We can learn a lot from Mary's example in the urban youth ministry context as well. We tend to be very territorial—*my* ministry, what *we* do, etc. And the result is certain ministries that try to do everything. But we're not designed as humans to do everything! We must learn how to come together as brothers and sisters in the same city, and realize we are working toward the same mission.

JOSEPH AND MARY: FAITHFUL TO THE JEWISH CUSTOMS

"When they had completed everything according to the law of the Lord, they returned to Galilee, to their own town of Nazareth. The boy grew up and became strong, filled with wisdom, and God's grace was on Him." (Luke 2:39-40, HCSB)

From the moment of birth, a Jewish child is welcomed into the family of Israel with rituals and celebrations. According to the Talmud, it was the custom to plant a cedar tree when a boy was born and a pine tree when a girl was born. The cedar signified royal power and wealth and symbolized growth and strength; the pine tree signi-fied great endurance (Psalm 92:12, NLT). When the children grew up and were about to be married, their trees were cut down and branch-es from each tree were used to build the four poles of the *chuppah* or marriage canopy. The *chuppah* is very significant on the Jewish wedding day. It was designed to resemble Abraham and Sarah's tent, which, according to tradition, was open on all four sides so as to welcome visitors from all directions. What a powerful way to tell the story of every tribe and tongue (the four corners of the earth) being welcome at the marriage supper of the Lamb.

Can you imagine Joseph explaining to Jesus that as one particular cedar tree grew tall and strong that it had been planted on Jesus' be-half? This is just one example of the many Jewish customs that were formed into the heart and mind of the boy Jesus. Many of us learned customs as children, such as the importance of being friendly and greeting people, and that a good reputation (and a bad one, too) fol-lows you wherever you go. My mother used to tell us to treat people well "because God don't like ugly." Jewish boys learned numerous customs to teach them about Yahweh. And many of those customs have lasted for generations.

Stepping Up

I remember the baby dedications at New Creation Christian Fellowship of San Antonio, Texas. Bishop David M. Copeland and Dr. Claudette Copeland were sensitive to charge the parents, family, and church body as witnesses to the announcement that they were now account-able to see the child raised in the admonition of the Lord.

Wouldn't it be something if every church congregation took this custom seriously? What a powerful statement to local communities for the individuals in the church to make themselves available to assist parents, especially single parents, in raising their children in a godly way. Why shouldn't social service agencies refer families to the church and the church be prepared to serve them, as this vow is made manifest in our lives and ministries? Well, I believe we're coming to that place, and the church should take this step. And what can the church do? Anything it has to do! Does your church have a kitchen? Then you prepare meals. Do you have resources to offer others? Then step up and make it happen. Serve. It's time. Are we really who we say we are? Do we want a coffee shop in our church lobby as a safe haven, or do we care more about ministering to the real needs of our communities?

The Lasting Impact of Parental and Community Instruction

"Teach a youth about the way he should go; even when he is old he will not depart from it." (Proverbs 22:6, HCSB)

Parental instruction and training has been proven to have a lasting impact in the psychosocial development of a child. The early years of a child's life are when learning is crucial. It's good to know that the Jewish culture of Mary and Joseph's day can teach us about the community's involvement in training up a child. To Hebrew parents the Torah held instructions for the mother and father to give to their children as they instructed them in matters of living and warned them about morally dangerous situations.

Adam Clarke gives us some insight as he comments on the text of Proverbs 22:6:

> "Initiate the child at the opening (the mouth) of his path." When he comes to the opening of the way of life, being able to walk alone, and to choose; stop at this entrance, and begin a series of instructions, how he is to conduct himself in every step he takes. Show him the duties, the dangers, and the blessings of the path; give him directions how to perform the duties, how to escape the dangers, and how to secure the blessings, which all lie before him.

The instruction given in Deuteronomy stands out as the most important concept for comprehensive teaching and training of children (Deuteronomy 4:44; Deuteronomy 6:1-8). Many of the words used in the text refer to the law being perpetuated in and through the generational family lines. Deuteronomy 6 shows us how this takes place: "[Do this] so that you may fear the Lord your God all the days of your life by keeping all His statutes and commands I am giving you, your son, and your grandson, and so that you may have a long life" (Deuteronomy 6:2, HCSB).

Science has revealed that children's ability to learn something new is based on the number of experiences they have with a concept. Deuteronomy 6:6-9 reveals the processing concepts of learning, reinforcement, and repetition:

> These words that I am giving you today are to be in your heart. Repeat them to your children. Talk about them when you sit in your house and when you walk along the road, when you lie down and when you get up. Bind them as a sign on your hand and let them be a symbol on your forehead. Write them on the doorposts of your house and your gates. (HCSB)

It's interesting to note that the parent was to repeat the words of the Torah to his or her children and talk about them as they sat in the house and walked along the road. The reinforcement is taking place because the young person and his instructor would be spending time together in familiar places. And familiarity triggers a memory of the words and concepts learned.

Imagine a parent or older sibling walking down the road with a child. As they came upon a stream, there would be a place of instruction. The conversation might go something like this:

Adult: "There is a river whose streams make glad the city of God." (Psalm 46:4) Then the adult takes the young person by the hand and says: "Every stream is fed by a river; and when the stream reaches a city like ours, the people are happy because we have a source of water."

Child: "Our city isn't called 'God.'"

Adult: "You're right. But what I want you to understand is that you and I are like a city that belongs to God."

Child: "Oh, so we can be glad because we have a stream?"

Adult: "Not only because we have a stream, but also because God is to us like the river is to the stream—like the river gives water to the stream, God gives us life."

Child: "There is a river whose streams make glad the city of God. Hmmm…" Then after a short pause, the child begins to skip and sing: "He has made me glad! He has made me glad!"

Generative Community

The Hebrews' concept of Torah became associated with priestly instruction to the community, which resulted in the art of nurturing generative communities. (*Generative* refers to a way a culture maintains and passes on its identity to its children, such as storytelling, songs, and nursery rhymes.) In all of our lives, there is some sort of culture that maintains our identity. The Jewish community continues to pass on the Torah and other ancient writings of the Hebrew Bible (in other words, the wisdom of Solomon and the writings of the prophets) to the next generation. For us today, family, teachers, clergy, and community leaders use the Bible as they nurture others and maintain their way of life.

The adult nods and whispers, "That's it."

As an educator I was taught the significance of implementing association with reinforcement. In his book *How the Brain Learns*, David Sousa writes that the neurons in a child's brain make many more connections than the neurons in adult brains. And a newborn's brain makes connections at an incredible pace as he or she absorbs the environment. The richer the environment, the greater the number of connections made; consequently, learning can take place faster and with greater meaning. This process continues throughout our lives, but it appears to be the most intense between the ages of 3 and 12.

In his hometown of Nazareth, Jesus was learning and growing like any other Jewish boy at that time. Experiences were shaping his brain and designing the unique patterns that would influence how he handled future experiences while worshiping in the synagogue, learning a trade with Joseph, and other important endeavors.

But in order to talk about the Scriptures and walk a young person through a text means that we need to be well acquainted with the Scriptures—and be willing to walk with young people until they have a basic understanding. If we don't know the Scriptures well enough to do this, then we need to find a way to gain understanding. Only then can we seize a teachable moment. For example, when riding the T (public transit) with a young person, listen for the promised voice of the Holy Spirit to point ways to truth and Scripture. If we have eyes to see and ears to hear, we can find God in all things—even on the train or in the neighborhood.

A long time ago I did some work in Pine Bluff, Arkansas, with Kids Across America. One day I went shopping for shoes with an African-American sophomore girl. When we got to the store, I noticed a pair I wanted on the display rack, and I asked the clerk for a discount. We bantered back and forth, but the girl I was with was becoming really uncomfortable—as I asked to speak with the manager, she put the hood on her jacket over her head. I didn't get the discount, but it turned into a very teachable moment with my young friend—that we're accountable for what we do with our money. I told her, "*Display* means *dis-count* or you don't get *dis-money.*" (That finally made her laugh.) But an important lesson about stewardship came from an everyday activity.

Circumcision Significance

"The boy grew up and became strong, filled with wisdom, and God's grace was on Him." (Luke 2:40, HCSB)

Dr. Luke repeats this statement in Luke 2:52, but now in the present progressive tense: "And Jesus *kept increasing* in wisdom and stature, and in favor with God and men" (*emphasis added*, NASB).

From the day Jesus was born, he began to grow just like you and I do—physically, emotionally, socially, and spiritually. Sometimes we forget that Jesus of Nazareth was God come *in the flesh*. Every day of his childhood, Jesus had to grow and develop and learn the customs of his community like any other Hebrew boy. And it all started eight days after Jesus' birth: "When the eight days were completed for His circumcision, He was named JESUS—the name given by the angel before He was conceived" (Luke 2:21, HCSB).

The covenant of circumcision came from God's commandment to Abram. "This is My covenant, which you are to keep, between Me and you and your offspring after you: Every one of your males must be circumcised" (Genesis 17:10, HCSB). During an infant's circumcision, before the blade touches the skin, the *mohel* (the official of the ceremony) or the father recites the blessing for circumcision: "Blessed are you Adonai our God, Ruler of the Universe, who has sanctified us with Your commandments and commanded us to bring him into the covenant of Abraham, our father." This tradition identified the newborn male as a part of the covenant of Abraham. It was also announced that the boy would begin to learn the Torah, and then a prayer of being set apart was recited.

The cutting procedure signifies cutting away impure things—and Paul took it a step further when he wrote to the church at Colosse: "You were also circumcised with the circumcision made without hands, by putting off the body of the sins of the flesh, by the circumcision of Christ" (Colossians 2:11, NKJV). This helps us to understand our identity in Christ. Our hearts are circumcised as new believers, and we step into our own sanctification process. The cutting away signifies our willingness to live a distinctively different life from those who don't honor and live for *Adonai* Almighty God. In other words, just as the Hebrew boys were born into and circumcised into the Jewish culture, when we become born again (a child of God), we're born into and circumcised into the culture of the kingdom of God.

What that means for urban youth ministry is that we need to be speaking into the lives of teenagers who've been crucified with Christ along with us (and we ourselves need mentors speaking into our lives). The bottom line is that you *know* and are *known* in the deepest ways possible so positive spiritual growth can be given every opportunity to occur.

There's also significance for us in regard to the announcement that's made about the infant learning the Torah. We, too, must be committed to teaching the Word to newborns in Christ. Yet, there's a difference between teaching and preaching. Teaching involves dialogue, demonstration, and application; preaching involves heralding something (and you're the only one talking). Kids are so tired of being *talked at* and *talked to*—instead they want to interact. So we must work hard to encourage them accordingly...and without dictating. Remember: Teaching can have reaching power when we talk to marginalized teenagers who come to Christ and tell them they have a new identity. For example, could we use the powerful illustration of circumcision and teach them that the number eight means new beginnings and that circumcision on the eighth day represents a new beginning now that Christ has circumcised their hearts?

Community Agreement in the Destiny of the Child Called Jesus
Scripture tells us that Simeon was a "righteous and devout" man and "the Holy Spirit was upon him" (Luke 2:25). Here's the first wit-

ness who wouldn't see death until he'd seen the Messiah. Guided by the Spirit, Simeon entered the temple. When Mary and Joseph brought the baby Jesus to present him to God, Simeon held the infant and praised God. Mary and Joseph were in awe of all that was said about Jesus. Then Simeon went on to tell Mary, "Indeed, this child is destined to cause the fall and rise of many in Israel and to be a sign that will be opposed—and a sword will pierce your own soul—that the thoughts of many hearts may be revealed" (Luke 2:34-35, HCSB).

Too often we want to protect youth from God-ordained difficulties that are predesigned for their character training. God knows our end before our birth, and often God allows certain experiences, even difficult ones, to shape us into the image of his Son. When parents are going through difficult times with their children, God in his sovereignty may send others in their community of believers to speak encouragement to the parents, letting them know that this difficult season in their children's lives is a part of the purposed plan of preparation for their calling and mission.

The second witness in the temple was Anna, the prophetess who had devoted herself completely to the Lord's service in the temple. An old woman well past her 80th birthday, she testified to all who were looking forward to the redemption of Jerusalem that the Messiah had come. Can we do any less in our positions as urban youth workers?

God chose to speak through Simeon and Anna to confirm Jesus' identity, and God also allowed Mary and Joseph to be encouraged by Simeon and Anna's God-given affirmations. These were words of assurance; surely this is the Son of God! This Jewish couple was chosen of God to raise *The Child* in their home in Nazareth according to their customs. (In later chapters we'll discuss the power of a custom.)

TRAINING UP

The Deuteronomy Scripture shared earlier in this chapter is the essence of the parental role in education: *Teach them as you are coming and going, as you stand up and sit down.* The Words of God were to be taught, talked about, and used in worship to declare symbolically that they were a part of the people's very being.

Parental and community roles in training up a child were part of God's plan from the beginning. Each parent was allotted a role in the raising of children, according to classic Jewish literature. Education for both boys and girls was the mother's responsibility for the first three years. This was generally when weaning would take place. She then taught the girls domestic duties throughout their childhood. From age three and beyond, boys were taught the laws of Moses by their fathers. And the fathers were also responsible for teaching their sons a trade, while girls were allowed to take professional jobs. (This could be why the Proverbs 31 woman was recognized as a businesswoman!)

The intent of education was always to point the young person to the precepts of God. Children were to understand the nature of God through what God had done and what was required in the law.

Parents are the first ones called to nurture a child. Parents and those serving in that role are positioned to lay foundations that will be set as neurological patterns and connections in their children's minds. And just as Jesus learned to rely on the Holy Spirit dwelling inside him to be his internal Teacher, we're also called to train our children to seek the guidance of the Holy Spirit to teach and remind them of everything that God has taught them.

Jesus is also our example in terms of walking out day-to-day lessons of growth and development. At the age of 12, Jesus understood who his real Father was. He said to Mary, "Did you not know that I must be about my Father's business?" (Luke 2:49, NKJV) Jesus reminded his mother of what she'd probably told him about his destiny when he was still a little boy.

TEACHING PURPOSE AND DESTINY

Adults have a tendency to speak about only what we know is happening in a young person's life as opposed to speaking words of *purpose* and *destiny*. I believe that as mentors and models, those of us investing in the lives of children and youth must be willing to listen for and learn the precepts of the Lord in order to find creative ways to teach them to the next generation.

We must be careful as we raise up young people to make sure we're creating environments that are conducive to them hearing the voice of God and learning to walk in obedience. Within our communities is where they'll learn and grow to know the praises of the Lord's might and the wonderful works he has performed, is performing, and will perform (Psalm 78:4).

DR. RENÉ'S PRESCRIPTION
for Seeking and Strengthening Family Models

- Fight against compartmentalization
- Find ways to serve parents of your students
- Learn from those who've been through the hardest times
- Admit that you can't go it alone
- Champion parenting as a holy office
- Encourage teaching in everyday moments
- Dialogue with teenagers rather than talk at them
- Don't fear difficulties in students' lives
- Emphasize a young person's purpose and destiny

Rx

QUESTIONS FOR DISCUSSION

1. In many urban communities there are numerous teenage parents and grandparents under the age of 30. These are young people who in some cases haven't fully matured emotionally, psychologically, or socially. The challenge for us as youth workers is to recognize patterns of misfortune that are a result of inexperience and knowledge. *What are some things you can do to better identify these areas of "immaturity"?*

2. The laws of science tell us that maturity is a prerequisite to multiplication. In the same way, God told Adam and Eve be *fruitful* first and then to multiply. How can we encourage young people to be more productive with their teenage years? Think about youth who've been entrusted to your care in the urban community, then make a list of things that can be done at home or ways they can learn more life skills and work skills to better their future.

3. We must be aware that our cultural upbringings can affect the ways we view the teenagers to whom we're assigned. Therefore we must listen to and learn about the community and culture of the youth in the cities we're called to minister in. Write down your basic understanding of the role family plays *through the eyes of the youth.* (If you're not sure, the best way to know is to ask your students.)

4. After you've interviewed a few youth to learn how they perceive the role of the family in their lives, take some time to meet the elders of your community and ask them the same question: *What do you believe is the role of the family in the lives of teenagers?* Record your results.

5. What does Scripture tell you about God being to each of us a provider, protector, and pardoner? In other words, how does God being our Heavenly Father and the body of Christ being our family fulfill what could be missing in all of our lives?

CHAPTER THREE

MODELS IN THE SYNAGOGUE
LEADERS IN THE NEIGHBORHOOD

Two words that come to mind when I think of a synagogue are *community* **and** *culture.*

Community because the synagogue was (and is) a gathering of people with common unity; *culture* because a particular people group had a distinct way of coming together in the synagogue that set them apart from others.

COMING FACE TO FACE WITH ANOTHER KIND OF SYNAGOGUE

In the fall of 2006, I was fortunate to take a mission trip to South Africa and Botswana. One afternoon after we'd served the women and children medically, spiritually, and emotionally, we all walked about a half-mile down the road to what appeared to be a common gathering place. It was about 4:30 in the afternoon, and people began to fill this meeting place. There were women carrying babies, teens, children, and several others returning from work. They all joined the tribe leaders and ministers of the community in song, prayer, and proclamation of thanksgiving.

This setting resembled the closest thing in my mind to what historians call an ancient synagogue. Why? Because everyone from the local tribe came together under one roof; that place was where teaching happened and where information and celebration occurred. It's much the same with the synagogue: It's where the people of the community came together to hear what was forth-coming. And there was prayer. Praise. Teaching. Announcement and proclamation and celebration.

In the last 20 years or so, most noted youth ministry experts and scholars on urban youth ministry (and urban youth workers them-selves) have been my Caucasian brothers and sisters—along with a handful of people of color known for their longevity in hands-on inner-city youth ministry. In fact, numbers of suburban white broth-ers and sisters have "relocated" to urban communities to "serve the poor," and in the process they've raised millions of dollars, built cen-ters, and launched sports leagues, tutoring programs, and Bible clubs. I'm appreciative of their efforts and commitment—but I believe God is also anointing and empowering authentic, indigenous leaders in the communities of the city. Most African American and Hispanic and Latino youth workers are known for their ability to preach, teach, and train—and God is raising them up.

It's important that we seek them out and make room for them. Primarily because, as with the synagogue community, these leaders-to-be are part of the local church, the local community of believers. Those in authority have had the chance to watch them grow and mature, week in, week out, as part of a spiritual tribe. They see their talents and abilities emerging. And all that combined simply makes for a leader more in tune with the needs of the urban community.

Not long ago I heard an African preacher share this statement: "Empowerment is not just about money; it is a way of thinking." Lead-ers, and especially those of us from marginalized populations, have been given a mandate to walk as captains over God's inheritance! It's humbling to know that God has entrusted a generation to our care. We must believe there is greatness in the youth of our cities and be willing to encourage and prepare them with the necessary tools to walk in greatness.

WHERE PREPARATION STARTS

History shows us how children of royalty are trained and prepared before they actually sit in the position to rule. Matthew writes of the journey to the cross and then the throne of our Lord and Savior Jesus Christ.

> Now after Jesus was born in Bethlehem of Judea in the days of Herod the king, magi from the east arrived in Jerusalem, saying, "Where is He who has been born King of the Jews?" (Matthew 2:1-2, NASB)

Jesus was born a king, but he didn't take his rightful place until after he'd grown in all respects and learned obedience to God through the things he suffered—just as we do. Jesus journeyed on earth and was trained in order to reign. Throughout Jesus' childhood, teenage years, and early adulthood, men and women nurtured him until who he was on the inside was called to manifest outwardly to the world that he indeed is the King.

In the same way, you and I must trust the workings of the Spirit of God to use whomever God has designed to carry out Christ's mission in the city. Because you've never seen a youth ministry function in this way before, or because it comes in a different package than you're used to, you must keep in mind this advice from Dr. Janet Hale: "Different does not mean deficient."

SYNAGOGUES IN THE COMMUNITY

The Greek term *synagogue*, which means "to gather," is used throughout the New Testament and in the writings of Josephus and rabbinic sources to refer to a Jewish community or building. It differed from the temple in that it had no altar, and prayer and the reading of the Torah took the place of the animal sacrifice. In addition to being a place of prayer, the synagogue performed an important social function. It became the cradle of an entirely new type of social and religious life and established the foundation for a religious community of universal scope.

The importance of the synagogue for Judaism cannot be over-estimated. More than any other institution, it gave character to the Jewish faith. This is the place where the Israelites learned the inter-pretation of the law.

According to Ezekiel 11:16, God identifies himself as a sanctuary: "Although I sent them far away among the nations and scattered them among the countries, yet for a little while I have been a sanctuary for them in the countries where they have gone." In addition, this verse was interpreted by Jewish authorities to mean that in worldwide dis-persion, Israel would have synagogues as smaller replicas to replace the loss of the temple in Jerusalem. Indeed synagogues were located in all parts of the land, and they put the people in touch with their religious leaders. And during difficult circumstances (such as their enslavement in Egypt, exile in Babylon, and Roman occupation), the Jews knew to cry out to Yahweh as a people group gathered in community.

In the same way, for years in small rural towns and among certain people groups, the local church was the gathering place for town meetings. And the church was considered to be one of the four pil-lars of the African-American community: Church, family, education, and empowerment. The history of many African-American churches is also embedded in justice. Coming together meant a time for pray-ing, singing, and becoming of one mind for a strategic plan of action in the community.

Still, Jesus taught his disciples that the heart of God was never to build a temple or external edifice for the people to commune with God. Solomon's speech at the completion of the temple gives us some insight into the purpose of the building project:

"Blessed *be* the Lord God of Israel, who spoke with His mouth to my father David, and with His hand has fulfilled *it*, saying, 'Since the day I brought My people out of Egypt, I have chosen no city from any tribe of Israel *in which* to build a house, that My name might be there; but I chose David to be over my people Israel.' Now it was in the heart of my father David to build a temple for the name of the Lord God of Israel. But the Lord said to my father David, 'Whereas it was in your heart to build a temple for My name, you did well that it was in your heart.'" (1 Kings 8:15-18, NKJV, emphasis added)

It was David's desire to build a temple for the Lord's name, and God honored it. But God desired not a temple for his name to dwell there, *but for a human* to bear his name. A temple built by human hands will one day be destroyed, but the Spirit of the Living God who resides in the hearts and minds of people will live forever. Jesus told his disciples that the temple in Jerusalem would be destroyed (Matthew 24:1-2). Then 36 years after Jesus' death, resurrection, and ascension, the temple *was* destroyed. When speaking of his earthly body, Jesus said, "Destroy this temple, and in three days I will raise it up" (John 2:19, NKJV). And in his letter to the church at Corinth (which was

A Typical Synagogue Service

Those qualified were permitted to conduct the services (Christ in Matthew 4:23 and Luke 4:14-16; Paul in Acts 13:13-15). The Sabbath was the appointed day for public worship (Acts 15:21). According to Edersheim, the Mishnah (Megillah 4.3) indicates that the service consisted of five parts. First, the Shema was read. This prayer covers Deuteronomy 6:4-9; 11:13-21; and Numbers 15:37-41. Then synagogical prayers were recited, the most ancient and best known being the 18 petitions and benedictions.

The following prayers are still read in King James English in most African-American traditional churches, too. There's still an order of service and a reverence for the Word. These were the prayers that Jesus grew up hearing and reciting. As he grew into adulthood and began his three-year ministry, these very Scriptures and prayers were recited—but now in the power of the Spirit. I've found that young people don't mind the order in the house of the Lord if they understand its meaning.

The first of the Eighteen Benedictions reads: "Blessed art Thou, the Lord our God, and the God of our fathers, the God of Abraham, the God of Isaac, and the God of Jacob: the great, the mighty and the terrible God, the most high God Who showest mercy and kindness, Who createst all things, Who rememberest the pious deeds of the patriarchs, and wilt in love bring a redeemer to their children's children for Thy Name's sake; O King, Helper, Saviour and Shield! Blessed art Thou, O Lord, the Shield of Abraham."

Another prayer (the Fourteenth Benediction) is worded: "And to Jerusalem, Thy city, Thou wilt return in mercy and wilt dwell in her midst, as Thou hast said. And do Thou build her soon in our days an eternal building, and the throne of David Thou wilt speedily establish in the midst of her."

The restoration of Israel to the land of their fathers, the return of the Shekinah glory to the Temple and rebuilt city of Jerusalem, and the reestablishment of the Davidic dynasty are recurring themes in the prayers.

These were followed by the reading of the Law. The Pentateuch, which is now read in the synagogues in annual cycles, was originally covered in three years. After the reading from the first portion of the Old Testament Canon, a selection from the Prophets was read. In the time of Christ, this portion was not yet fixed, but the reader was permitted to make his own choice (Luke 4:16-18). The reading of Scripture was central. The portion of the Prophets was expounded, and an exhortation drawn from it. The benediction concluded the service. Later additions were the translation and exposition of the Scripture portions read. In order to conduct public worship in the synagogue, 10 adult males were required.

likely read in the Corinthian synagogue or in a home where followers of Christ gathered), Paul admonished the believers that their bodies were the temples of the Living God (1 Corinthians 6:19).

DON'T LET THE BUILDING ITSELF LEAD TO DIVISION

God was preparing his people to become living epistles known and read by all of humanity. Even today, our lives should be telling the story of a Living Savior. Many of the beautiful edifices—which we call churches—around the world today are to be gathering places of equipping so that the people who are the embodied Christ may bring the Spirit of God wherever they go. But sometimes the external trappings have led to division, classism, and discrimination.

The Gospels speak of the synagogues of Nazareth (Matthew 13:54; Luke 4:16) and Capernaum (Mark 1:21; John 6:59) as places where Jesus taught. According to the Talmud, it was required that synagogues be built on high ground or above surrounding houses. A common plan or design had a hall with columns at the edges of the floor and benches in tiers along each wall. There was usually a cupboard to house the scrolls of the Law and the Prophets. For the readings, the scrolls would be carried to a reading desk or raised platform (*bemá*) in the center of the hall. In later synagogues the *bemá* often lay against one wall, facing Jerusalem. Seats near the reading desk were for the more honorable (Matthew 23:6). James warns against this, saying:

> My brethren, do not hold the faith of our Lord Jesus Christ, *the Lord* of glory, with partiality. For if there should come into your assembly a man with gold rings, in fine apparel, and there should also come in a poor man in filthy clothes, and you pay attention to the one wearing the fine clothes and say to him, "You sit here in a good place," and say to the poor man, "You stand there," or, "Sit here at my footstool," have you not shown partiality among yourselves, and become judges with evil thoughts? (James 2:1-4, NKJV)

May it not be so in our time and on our watch.

SLOWING DOWN (AND WISING UP)

I've been affiliated with parachurch organizations for the last 25 years, and I've witnessed the launching of numerous urban ministry departments and teams. Some are doing an excellent job, and others are struggling with prematurely launched ministries with limited knowledge of their community's history, specifically in regard to unresolved issues and frustration with the local church. For example, consider a leader who comes onboard a parachurch team but has just left a church or ministry background where he experienced spiritual abuse and hasn't begun the process of healing; he's vulnerable to being a wounded healer who's likely to wound others rather than one who's being made whole and ministering healing to the wounded.

Unlike the synagogues of old, the urban parachurch is often rushed into existence without much thought, prayer, or consideration—and issues like the latter example crop up more frequently for those very reasons. Furthermore, the urban parachurch that's rushed into existence lacks the benefit of a shared vision grounded in community—something the synagogue has in droves. Have you sought out elders in the community before launching your ministry? Are you taking time to ask the questions that need asking? (For example, "Why has there been a barrier between the church and parachurches for the last 30 years in this neighborhood?") Have you taken the time to show the community your heart before you give them your vision?

In addition, instead of joining what local churches are already doing, parachurches tend to do their own thing—and that has pastors very frustrated. Because *para* means "to come alongside," not to be or do everything. Which is why the church isn't always willing to embrace what the parachurch is doing; often churches believe parachurches are taking away their people. Instead we should come together and say, "You have a slammin' discipleship program, and we have a great leadership ministry—can we join forces?" Let's let the body be the body! We're too territorial. We're all trying to be these individual bodies instead of one corporate, united front. If you teach, then teach. If you sing, then sing. We need to start getting down to business and embrace the gifts of the body so that the believers can be equipped and trained to serve in the community. Otherwise we'll just become more and more isolated. And do you know what happens when you become isolated? You die lonely.

And beyond that, what are *you* doing to get fed personally? So many youth workers—urban and otherwise—are suffering spiritually because they pour their lives into so many kids, but no one's pouring their lives into them. Where are you getting nurtured? This is so crucial. Especially when you're involved in high-pressure ministry ventures. You have to have people around you—I call them "stretcher bearers"—to carry you to Jesus when you're injured on your spiritual journey.

SYNAGOGUE DUTIES

The synagogue, like the church in the neighborhood, was a place of local Jewish autonomy, yet it was subject to Roman law. Each congregation's elders were empowered to exercise discipline and at times excommunication. According to Witty, the *ruler* of the synagogue supervised the service to see that it was carried on in accord with tradition. The *attendant* had a few responsibilities; he would bring the scrolls of Scripture for reading, and later replace them in the ark of the covenant. He was also responsible for *instructing the children to read.* The *dispenser of alms* received the money from the synagogue and distributed it to people in need. (Now we understand why Jesus was put out by those who would give very little when a widow gave all she had; someone who was probably in great need herself was willing to give her offering to the Lord for the sake of others.) Finally, a *competent interpreter* was required to paraphrase the Law and the Prophets into the vernacular Aramaic. In Jesus' day there was a generation who attended synagogue who had grown up learning the Aramaic language. Most weren't proficient in the Hebrew dialect.

OUR DUTIES TODAY

In our urban youth ministries, we need interpreters and teachers. The percentage of young people who cannot read is at an all-time high, not to mention biblical illiteracy. And the languages and dialects spoken in many cities of the United States aren't typically used in most churches today. To effectively reach the young people in these cities, it will take teachers who are filled with the Spirit of God modeling God's truth through relationships. And we cannot underestimate the power of prayer. God desires to move in the hearts of young people everywhere.

In Acts 4:31, it says that when the followers of Jesus finished praying, the place they were in was shaken and they were filled with the Holy Spirit and began to speak the Word of God with great boldness.

Boldness here is better interpreted as "confidence." We, too, need the confidence to believe that God is who he says he is, and that God will do what he says he'll do.

We have an opportunity to accurately speak the text (the Bible) in a relevant language and proper context. We must ask God to guard our hearts and not allow us to get caught in a people-pleasing trap of using "hip-hop" language to impress and keep a crowd. Too many young people are getting fired up and "crunk" for Christ, but they have no sustaining power once the hype is over. Have we given them true bread to eat? Jesus modeled to the disciples to set the people down in groups before you feed them (Mark 6:39; Luke 9:14). We seat the multitudes and feel so excited because we filled the auditorium that we merely entertain them and leave them malnourished. This must end.

For years the local church in most urban communities was used as a gathering place for the people of the community. The strength of urban ministry within a community—and namely the church—is that the body of Christ becomes the family of God to those in the congregation. Once again we need to let the church become the community-gathering place and come alongside the family to help empower, equip, and raise the next generation.

DR. RENÉ'S PRESCRIPTION

for Harnessing the Help of the Neighborhood

- Strive for the kind of community manifested in ancient synagogues
- Slow down and listen for God's leading
- Seek the counsel of local spiritual elders
- Join forces with other ministers and end your isolation

QUESTIONS FOR DISCUSSION

1. It's critical to check what motivates us in ministry. Are we more motivated and moved by the cause, the injustices, human abuses, or needing to be involved in fixing what's wrong? Or are we more motivated by the Spirit of God to follow through with our God-ordained assignment? Generally, where there is passion for something, there is vision for it as well. Write down your passions for urban youth ministry. Has God given you a vision as to how these passions can be met? Take some time to scribe your vision for meeting the specific needs in the community.

2. Does your ministry outreach tend to divide or unify other helping/service providers in the community? Cause-oriented ministries can compartmentalize the notions of who deserves help and who doesn't in others' minds. How can your loving concern and desire for unity cover over divisions?

3. Often our passion for Christ can easily turn into a passion for ministry and "the cause." This shift will eventually displace God as the center of your outreach. How can you keep your focus on intimacy with God and avoid building with your hands what's not in your heart?

4. Read Luke 2:39-52. Is God's timing always perfect? A zeal for causes can propel us into program implementation prematurely. Scripture tells us that Jesus recognized his call at the age of 12 but waited another 18 years to begin his intense discipleship relationships and teaching ministry. In what ways are you tempted to rush your outreach?

5. First things first: Is your priority to grow more in love with the Lord? Paul shared with the church at Corinth that they have not seen nor heard all that God has in store for those who love him (1 Corinthians 2:9-10). Paul writes that he counts all things as loss in view of the surpassing value of knowing Christ Jesus (Philippians 3:8). What can you do to keep your focus clear and energized by love?

CHAPTER FOUR

ON-THE-JOB TRAINING
LESSONS FROM THE LEADERS

Whoever does not teach his son a trade
is as if he brought him up to be a robber.
—rabbinical saying

One afternoon while my mother was helping my eight-year-
old nephew, Aaron, with his homework, she mentioned something about a young man not having a job. Not even looking up from his work, my nephew said, "I guess he won't eat." My mother, shocked, asked him what he'd said, and Aaron went on to explain that the Bible says, "If a man doesn't work, he should not eat." Upon invoking 2 Thessalonians 3:10, my nephew continued in conversation about how difficult it would be if you didn't have a job to help him pay for groceries. Aaron had been hearing my sister share much of what she heard when we were young: "I need to get to the job so we can pay the bills and have food on the table." "Money doesn't grow on trees."

This summer, while celebrating my mother's birthday with the family, I learned how these sayings and many more were spoken in my grandmother's house. Sitting around the kitchen table after the Sunday evening meal, I laughed, listened, and learned from my mother and her two younger siblings, John and Catherine, about the origin of their work ethic and persistence—specifically in reference to my grandmother's laundry business way back when.

Uncle John is "the philosopher"—there's always a comment and lesson in much of what he brings to the table. "Yeah, Sarah Bryant [my grandmother: "Big Ma"] didn't play when it came to getting the food on the table and getting your work done."

Then Aunt Catherine chimed in and spoke in the tone of my grandmother, *"John, get up and get moving—you need to pick up the clothes and get them back here so we can get to them."*

Uncle John continued, "I learned as a boy how to launder clothes. I take nothing to the cleaners, and I still clean, starch, and press them."

My mother added, "Oh yeah, it was a system. Catherine had to get the fire going to heat the water. And my job was to make the starch and get the right amount poured into the bins for heavy, medium, or light, and then start ironing." The siblings listened to each other share with nods of affirmation and every now and then an "Amen!"

My younger sister Patricia and I would crack up when they imitated "Big Ma" giving instructions. Uncle John noted, "Mamma would make sure we were in place to do our jobs, and then she'd head out to clean the white folks' houses."

Patricia said, "Hey, that's good business. She was workin' the delegation."

I was humbled by how they joked, yet I knew the value of what they'd learned about working as a family to meet every need. God had given this widow and mother of 10 children the wisdom and fortitude to train up her children well. Ms. Sarah Bryant's laundry business was full of good management and detailed operations. There was a protocol, and everyone knew what it was and what it took to get the job done well:

Phase 1: My Uncle John, the youngest boy, picked up the clothes. He sometimes had to ride the streetcar and bus to get to the houses in the white neighborhoods. He shared how frustrating—and sometimes embarrassing—it was to have the dirty clothes in his lap as he sat between the other passengers.

Phase 2: While he was picking up the clothes, my Aunt Catherine, the youngest girl, was chopping wood with Big Ma or an older brother (before he left for work) to start the fire to heat the water.

Phase 3: My mother, Bernice, made the starch. As she said, she filled the bins, got the washboard wash, starched (light, medium, or heavy), and then ironed. If the more wealthy families had dropped off their curtains, then those were put on a curtain stretcher before they were ironed.

Phase 4: The clothes were delivered back to the customers.

Everyone in the Bryant house understood "together we'll get the job done."

Likewise, Solomon tells us: "Two *are* better than one, because they have a good reward for their labor" (Ecclesiastes 4:9, NKJV). Coming from what many would call a poor home, my grandmother, my mother, and her siblings continued to work diligently with their hands (Proverbs 10:4). Time meant money, and money meant bills paid and food on the table. My mother often spoke these words she heard as a child to my sister and me: "We can't afford for our work to be done poorly; we don't have the time to do it over again."

WHERE IS PRIDE IN WORK TODAY?

Have we forgotten the purpose of work? God told the first man and woman to be fruitful (in other words, *productive*) and *then* multiply. I believe we forget about the "fruitful" part and jump right into the "multiply" mandate. To be fruitful is to be productive. And to be productive takes discipline and effort—i.e., a good work ethic. So in urban youth ministry, we can get jobs for kids—but if they have a bad work ethic, those jobs won't be theirs for long. Because of what my mother taught me, I laundered my own clothes right through graduate school. (And now that times are tight again, I'm back at it!) And how do we get this across to kids? Sure, let them do their hip-hop and dancing, but then ask, "Can you fold clothes?" Help them find out about the little things that everybody needs—that keep life sustainable—and see if they can get jobs by doing them.

The dignity of honest work was clearly evident in the Epistles. At Corinth, Paul searched for work. He stayed with Priscilla and Aquila, who were also tentmakers, and worked with them (Acts 18:1-3). Paul continued to work so he wouldn't be a burden to the church, stating that it was his great "reward" to "make the gospel of Christ without charge" (1 Corinthians 9:18, KJV). Paul readily worked to be sure that his preaching would not be hindered.

According to Jewish culture, rabbis believed there was merit in every craft. And in today's culture, we must encourage young people that their jobs—whatever they put their hands to in order to provide for their families—have merit. We can learn much from Rabbi Meir: "Let a man always teach his son a cleanly and a light trade; and let him pray to Him whose are wealth and riches; for there is no trade which has not both poverty and riches, and neither does poverty come from the trade nor yet riches, but everything according to one's deserving (merit)." (Mishna [Kidd. iv. 14])

PERSEVERANCE

The Scriptures speak about tribulation producing perseverance and perseverance producing character (Romans 5:3-4). So what did the Bryant family persevere through? My mother and her siblings were children of the '40s. In the late 1940s and early '50s, things were a bit different than they are today for African Americans.

In his book *The Origins of the Civil Rights Movement*, Aldon D. Morris describes what life was like for black people, especially in the South prior to the 1960s. He speaks of a "tripartite system of domination" in which blacks were controlled economically, politically, and personally. The economic domination involved limiting blacks to the most menial jobs that paid the lowest wages. Morris reports that in the South in the 1950s, 75 percent of black males were unskilled laborers.

The political domination was twofold, Morris writes: It kept blacks from becoming voters, which in turn prevented anyone of color from holding any meaningful political office. For example, political positions all the way from the county sheriff to the entire criminal justice system were controlled by the dominant culture (whites), the members of which used their offices or positions to control blacks. Any attempts by blacks to resist or break out of their positions of powerlessness were met with brute force on every level, from law enforcement to the local thugs of the Ku Klux Klan.

My grandmother made sure her sons understood, "When you go over to *their* community, you're earning money for us to eat and get along in life." In that day if you were a man who showed any resistance (in the opinion of your accuser), you could be beaten, falsely accused, lynched, or in some cases disappear in a ditch. There was no place to turn for relief, except at home or in your own community. For many, the local church was where the pastor would speak words of encouragement to the weary souls of the African-American community who had endured a solid week of hearing abusive language and being treated as less than human from the time they walked out of their neighborhoods.

The personal domination that Morris refers to involved segregation and the emotional and psychological effects of being reminded— on a daily basis—of one's second-class status. My Uncle John shared what it was like to pick up the dirty and often smelly clothes and board a streetcar or a bus. Then, instead of sitting in the first available seat, he'd have to walk to the "colored section" to find one. So went the economics and politics of daily personal humiliation.

The civil rights movement and the removal of Jim Crow laws were first steps toward change, but they couldn't change everything—and certainly not overnight. The frame of mind of any people group is built into the infrastructure of its culture.

But this is one of the reasons why Jesus came—to get us thinking differently. His first words of ministry were "Repent, for the kingdom of heaven is at hand" (Matthew 4:17, NKJV). For those struggling in the midst of the civil rights movement, those words meant, "Change your way of thinking. There's a new culture, and in this culture there's no segregation, separatism, or sexism." My grandmother, although she didn't condone the behavior and belief system of a segregated world, taught her children there's One who's greater than all humans when she'd say, "God don't like ugly."

CHARACTER DEVELOPMENT
THROUGH THE GENERATIONS

To my grandmother, training and teaching children meant, among other things, shaping their thinking about why we work and how we work. The family business being passed from one generation to the next was not just about economics—minds were being shaped and character developed. It's about how you treat your customers, no matter what their ethnicity.

We must be keenly aware of any unhealthy mindsets being passed on from one generation to the next. Consider this example from 1 Samuel 16:6-10 (*The Message*):

> When they arrived, Samuel took one look at Eliab and thought, "Here he is! God's anointed!"
>
> But God told Samuel, "Looks aren't everything. Don't be impressed with his looks and stature. I've already eliminated him. God judges persons differently than humans do. Men and women look at the face; God looks into the heart."
>
> Jesse then called up Abinadab and presented him to Samuel. Samuel said, "This man isn't God's choice either."
>
> Next Jesse presented Shammah. Samuel said, "No, this man isn't either."
>
> Jesse presented his seven sons to Samuel. Samuel was blunt with Jesse, "God hasn't chosen any of these."

The rest of the passage speaks mightily to me. Samuel, after hearing God's voice, was persistent to do what was right in the eyes of the Lord and anoint the one who didn't "look the part." Leaders today have an opportunity to encourage and prepare the next generation of leaders to learn to wait on God and trust that God is able to raise up whomever God chooses.

David's father sent for him once Samuel had looked at and rejected Jesse's seven other sons. And when David walked up, God spoke again to Samuel: "Up on your feet! Anoint him! This is the one" (1 Samuel 16:12, *The Message*). Samuel immediately responded in obedience to the Lord, got his flask, and anointed David.

The word *anoint* has been so misused over time, so I don't want to focus too much on what it means as opposed to the manner and place where Samuel did it: This anointing ceremony in the house of Jesse was a public demonstration and announcement of God's chosen vessel. The Scripture says Samuel anointed David "with his brothers standing around watching" (v. 13). I see a twofold purpose in this occasion: One, David was being assured and released to be who he was purposed to be and accomplish what God had intended for him to accomplish. Second, those who didn't think David could possibly be the chosen representative were present for God's declaration and demonstration. *Selah.*

Then "the Spirit of God entered David like a rush of wind, God vitally empowering him for the rest of his life. Samuel left and went home to Ramah" (v. 13, *The Message*).

God empowered David to accomplish the work yet ahead. And we can rest assured that when we're leading a ministry to reach youth in the urban venues of the world, God already has in mind who's to take on the task. But remember, that person may not look like "the one" to our eyes. I know I didn't look like "the one," either. In the Jamaica Plain project I was leaning out windows and cussing at everybody, and in school I was an outcast and a target because others assumed I didn't have the capability to learn because of the color of my skin. After I became a believer, I tried hard to be used by God and spent my first eight years after college as a teacher. I didn't fit any mold of what "ministry" was supposed to be—I was just loving God and loving kids—yet doors started opening nonetheless. My experience should be an encouragement to any youth worker or teenager out there who doesn't "fit the mold," either.

THE EXAMPLE OF JESUS

"Is this not Joseph's son?" This is what the people in Jesus' hometown synagogue skeptically asked when Jesus began his public ministry in Nazareth. Luke 4:18 says Jesus opened with "The Spirit of the Lord is on me," and then finished the rest of the reading from the scroll of Isaiah, effectively describing himself as the Lord's servant who'd been anointed to preach good news to the poor, set the prisoners free, give sight to the blind, release the oppressed, and declare the acceptable year of the Lord. Jesus was 30 years old when he read this. And no one expected to witness what they did that day.

The folks who lived in Jesus' old neighborhood had no idea that the power of God rested in Jesus, the little boy they remembered. They expected Jesus to follow in the family business of carpentry. So how did he come to this place in his journey? Jesus' divine assignment began well before that day in the synagogue—it was purposed along with the foundations of the earth.

When Mary and Joseph returned to Nazareth from Egypt, Jesus was a small child. Joseph, the provider for the family, was probably anxious to get on with his carpentry business there. But during this time, Palestine struggled under the oppression of Rome. All income was taxed to fund the Roman government. More often than not, the Roman tax system propagated greed and dishonesty from the Jewish tax collectors. Workers were often frustrated after putting in so many hours every day, only to see much of it taken away for taxes. However, Joseph knew that it was by making yokes and ploughshares that he could best serve God. As a faithful learner of the law, Joseph knew the writings of Moses—and he knew that Jehovah had given his hands the ability to improve his life and the life of his family.

"Beware that you do not forget the Lord your God by not keeping His commandments, His judgments, and His statutes which I command you today, lest—when you have eaten and are full, and have built beautiful houses and dwell in them; and when your herds and your flocks multiply, and your silver and your gold are multiplied, and all that you have is multiplied; when your heart is lifted up, and you forget the Lord your God who brought you out of the land of Egypt, from the house of bondage...then you say in your heart, 'My power and the might of my hand have gained me this wealth.' And you shall remember the Lord your God, for *it is* He who gives you power to get wealth, that He may establish His covenant which He swore to your fathers, as *it is* this day." (Deuteronomy 8:11-14, 17-18, NKJV)

Jewish boys learned this passage at an early age as a reminder of God being their provision. It was instilled in them that they would display God's glory through the work of their hands. Joseph likely explained to Jesus how oxen are yoked together to bear the burden of the workload in the field. Jesus heard how a young, inexperienced ox is yoked with a mature ox to learn. Jesus would later use this same illustration as he encouraged his disciples to take on *his* yoke and learn from him about working in the harvest (Matthew 11:28-29).

I often encourage young men and women to ask the Lord to open the doors to relationships with those who've been down the road they want to go in urban ministry. Those who'll be yoked with them. Those they can shadow. Those who'll share with them their philosophies. Those who'll tell them how they've dealt with prejudice, with money issues, with the difficulties of discipleship. Those who'll encourage them. Those who'll ultimately show them what it means in urban youth ministry to deny oneself, take up the cross, and follow Jesus.

THE WORK AND THE WORKERS OF THE CITY

When we speak of urban ministry today, the question needs to be asked: *Urban ministry from whose perspective?* When searching for a blueprint of urban ministry, we should take time to learn from the people in the existing culture and community. Joseph and other grassroots community members in Nazareth had daily tasks that were woven into the fabric of their beings and their culture. In the same way, we can learn from the men and women who've been long-time urban community members and doing grassroots ministry there. Numerous churches in the city have a heart to reach the youth of their community. Why aren't they at the table of urban youth ministry planning? While I'm grateful for individuals who are sent to the city as missionaries, I believe we need to learn from the faithful men and women who've lived in urban neighborhoods and are committed to the youth of their community. In fact, smart and humble missionaries to the city will contact these folks when they want to learn about the neighborhoods to which they've been called.

You know who I mean: The matriarchs and patriarchs of the community—the neighborhood leaders. The people you learn about in your Urban Ministry 101 course. That could mean Mr. Ray who used to own the barbershop on Fifth Street. He'd be invited to lunch and asked to give guided tours for the "urban ministry director" and maybe a board member coming in to "scout out the land." But often while "the Mr. Rays" of the city have a heart for ministry and their communities, they're also blue-collar workers who can't give much of their time because they work such long hours. So then Mr. Ray is invited to *volunteer* at the new urban center—and the full-time staffers of many parachurch ministries serving in city neighborhoods don't match the faces of color that populate those neighborhoods.

What Is Required?
Please understand that I'm not disparaging my white brothers and sisters who work in urban youth ministry. God looks at the heart. Humans look at outward appearances. The point is that when you don't look like everybody else in a particular culture, you have to come with something more than experience or good ideas, because ultimately the first thing everyone will see is your outward appearance. It comes back to being anointed by God to complete a mission. And when you're anointed by God, it doesn't matter what color you are. God can use anyone, anywhere. Yet a lot of people in urban youth ministry

just went—they weren't sent. They were stirred, not called. When you know you've been called, you'll stand up to anything.

So...can you hang in there? Not in arrogance, but in humility. Micah 6:8 shows what the Lord requires of us: "To act justly and to love mercy and to walk humbly with your God." Is that at the forefront of the five-year plan? We need to know the community, too—especially its history. What's worked, what hasn't. Because when you don't know the history of place, it's very difficult to make a future there. And are we remembering that we're there to share the gospel...and then let God change people? Because they might not be ready for change—but that doesn't mean it's not God's will for you to be there and be part of his ultimate plan for the city—to tear down strongholds and negative thought patterns; to stand against faulty systemic order. Are you willing to go there?

Letting Go
When we're convinced that the ministry belongs to God and God alone, we're better able to release it into the hands of those living in the community—those whom God raised up to model, teach, and train the next generation about his goodness and grace. And how do we get convinced? How do we come to a point where we can let go and release it to others? We have to take the time to get back to the basics and spend time digging through the Scriptures with our group or our team. Jesus was with his "team" for three years and then left. Do we trust the same Holy Spirit whom Jesus sent to his followers at Pentecost to take care of those whom we want to leave in charge of our ministries? Do we trust our "system of ministry"—or the Spirit who should be stirring the ministry?

AWAKENING CRITICAL CONSCIOUSNESS
During the oral defense of my doctoral dissertation, the statistics professor on my committee asked, "René, how did Paulo Freire's

writings influence your model design?"

I paused for a few minutes to ponder why he'd ask that question, and then I proceeded to share why I was convinced Freire's philosophy of awakening a critical conscience among the people in their own communities is what's needed in urban intervention.

While in Brazil, Freire studied the role of *conscientização* (Portuguese for "conscientization" or "consciousness raising") among migrant farm workers. *Conscientização* refers to learning to perceive social, political, and economic contradictions and then taking action against the oppressive elements. Freire believed that by making it possible for people to enter the historical process as responsible individuals who know and act—in contrast to those who are known and acted upon—launches them into the search for self-affirmation. The awakening of critical consciousness then leads the way to the expression of social discontent. And I believe that's exactly what's needed in urban ministry, especially when it comes to working with youth.

Stating my rationale gave me the added incentive to finish my graduate studies with a mission to encourage and empower urban youth and leaders to rebuild their city walls.

Role Models Needed

The Jewish community during Jesus' teenage years afforded him the opportunity to be influenced by the men around him, especially Joseph. And the women of the town of Nazareth also served as role models and teachers for the children and youth of their community. That influence was vitally important, especially in light of Israel's occupation at the hands of the Romans. Jewish fathers were called by God to teach their children that they were chosen of God to be God's people, and everything they learned as a trade pointed them to their coming deliverer. So Jesus and other 12-year-old boys would have understood something about living in an oppressed culture.

The Disciples' On-the-Job Training

Jesus, who continued to model the message of God's kingdom to his disciples, introduced kingdom culture while drawing their attention to what they'd learned in the Jewish community. The types and shadows of God's personality and diversity were displayed in and through the life of Christ.

Jesus also allowed his disciples to work alongside him. In this way Jesus demonstrates to the presidents and executive directors of today's ministries—especially those called to minister in diverse communities—the importance of empowering young men and women in the communities they're called to serve. Too often "partnership" takes on the personality of a mercy mission outreach of a dominant culture rather than the collective efforts of people empowered by the Spirit of God to meet the needs of the youth and families in the community. This must not be so. That dynamic must be avoided in urban youth ministry at all costs.

Jesus displayed evidence of an early Hebrew education. And he developed his disciples' language and literacy of faith as well. Just as the rabbis of the day would test their disciples' knowledge and citation of the Torah, Jesus tested his followers in their interpretation of the Word so their competency in the language of the Word was a living experience. (Can you see a pattern here?) It is incumbent upon us as youth ministers to teach and train our students just as Jesus taught and trained his students.

Finally, Jesus modeled for his disciples what it meant to live out the Scriptures by showing them what careful and unprejudiced teaching and learning was all about. For example, the Jews of that day tended to show prejudice against anything and anybody having to do with the Gentiles. Yet, Jesus' mingling with Gentiles showed his lack of prejudice. Should we as leaders in the urban youth ministry landscape do any different?

JESUS AS OUR MENTOR

As believers we have the Bible as a reference, and in its pages we can witness how men and women wrestled through life's difficult situations. The power of Jesus' coming as a human model is that we have someone we can look to and relate to. The New Living Translation of Paul's letter to the Hebrews says, "This High Priest of ours understands our weaknesses, for he faced all of the same testing we do, yet he did not sin" (4:15). That's good news! We have a model who walked on earth as we do, was born into a family of low monetary means, grew up under the watchful eyes of his community, and learned his community's customs. Jesus displayed how we're all born into a family of a particular culture and ethnicity. And while he was living in a colonized community of the Roman government, Jesus never renounced the culture or customs of his community but fully embraced life as a young Jewish boy, teenager, and young adult. It should be the same for the kids we're working with in the urban landscape.

Has God Been Preparing You Spiritually?

Having a degree in cultural diversity or urban ministry doesn't equate to God's preparation and Holy Spirit workings. Even having a passion for the poor or being of the same cultural ethnic group doesn't prepare you for God's kingdom calling. Good intentions usually aren't enough. The question to consider is this: *Has God worked out of you whatever may hinder the message of Christ's nature and kingdom being modeled? Has the Spirit of God worked in you, prepared you, and molded into you what's needed to reach those God has called you to?*

David lets us know that before we can become a *human model* of God's ministry to a multicultural community, it must be birthed in us by a *supernatural work* of the Holy Spirit:

Create in me a clean heart, O God,
And renew a steadfast spirit within me.

Do not cast me away from Your presence,
And do not take Your Holy Spirit from me.
Restore to me the joy of Your salvation,
And uphold me by Your generous Spirit.
Then I will teach transgressors Your ways,
And sinners shall be converted to You.
(Psalm 51:10-13, NKJV)

No matter which people group we're called to serve, the process of salvation is the same. The heart of humankind needs a Deliverer, and his name is Jesus Christ. We'll be convincing to the degree by which we ourselves have been convicted and convinced by God. It starts with God—and then continues with our response.

DR. RENÉ'S PRESCRIPTION

for Working Smarter (and with More Humility)

- Teach fruitfulness before getting down to multiplication
- Continually strive for the renewing of your mind
- Emphasize character development
- Don't discount those youth who seem to lack visible potential
- Pray for God's anointing
- Give up the illusion of control

QUESTIONS FOR DISCUSSION

Paul told the people of Corinth that they have many teachers, but they don't have many fathers. As a high school teacher and a veteran of training urban youth workers, I've learned quite a bit about surrogate parenting. This word *surrogate* has a two-fold meaning: The first being a *substitute*, and second *a person deputized for another in a specific role*. These definitions assist us as we reflect on our roles as leaders called to train youth in the urban community.

If you're working directly with youth, it's helpful to keep in mind that you're a *substitute*. When a substitute teacher comes to serve in my absence, I'm fully aware of when they're stepping in and what they're authorized or *deputized* to do. My job is to prepare a lesson plan for the sub, so that he or she can step in and move the lesson forward; in my absence they're deputized (given the rightful authority) to run the class. With this concept in mind, answer the following questions:

1. Who have you learned from in order to step into a place of leadership with your students?

2. The good news is that the Holy Spirit enables and deputizes you spiritually, but there's also an entrusting from the elders in the community that needs to happen. How have you "prepared the way" with those living in the community so that you can join forces with them to meet the needs of the youth?

3. Who in the community is working with you to meet the needs of the youth?

4. Was a plan left for you to do ministry in the community? If so, how are you developing that plan to better serve the youth and families in the community?

81

5. Read Habakkuk 2:2-4. If you haven't already, you must take the time to scribe a vision for continued ministry to the oppressed in your city. Be prayerful, insightful (learn from those around you), and be patient.

CHAPTER FIVE

OBSERVANCE AND OBEDIENCE
LEARNING TO LIVE OUT
WHAT WE'VE BEEN TOLD

The progression of maturity in our beliefs is marked by how deeply we listen to what God has for us personally, and to what degree we allow God's voice to be the dominant one in our lives.

We read that in every stage of his life, Jesus chose to be obedient. When Jesus was 12, he could have been accepted into a rabbi program at the temple. But when his parents came after him, the Word says he submitted to his parents and returned home with them. Luke 2:51 says, "He continued in subjection to them"; and verse 52 says, "Jesus kept increasing in wisdom and stature, and in favor with God and men" (NASB).

Obedience to his parents established in Jesus the potential for a greater depth of growth and development. Jesus stayed in this relationship posture all his life. First in relationship to the authority of his parents, next in relationship to a synagogue teacher or rabbi teaching him the Torah, then in relationship to his earthly father in learning a trade, and finally in a continual submission to the will of his heavenly Father. The latter is the part that seems most difficult for us to emulate—especially if we're sent to a brand-new place that operates and believes differently than we do.

I learned in my youth that nothing was free and that "lack was the mother of invention." When things were financially tight in my family and I needed money for a track meet, I had to find some kind of work in order to earn the money for the trip. So I'd look around the community to see if there was something I could do to help someone in the neighborhood, letting him or her know that I needed to earn money for my track meet. Sometimes I delivered papers on my bike; other times I collected cans, raked leaves, helped pick up yards—all kinds of things so I could get to my purposed end. Then after becoming a follower of Christ and becoming familiar with the Bible, I wanted to learn what it had to say about how I should do things.

While working as a leader in a ministry organization, I was visiting with a staff member who hadn't raised enough funding for her ongoing ministry status. As I listened to her talk, all I could think about was what I did and heard when I was younger: "Lack is the mother of invention," and "You shall remember the Lord your God, for *it is* He who gives you power to get wealth" (Deuteronomy 8:18). So I asked about her major. She said it was social work and criminal justice. This young lady was volunteering at one of the state juvenile facilities to do Bible studies and meet with girls. Then I asked her a simple question: "Is there a job opening there?"

Before I got too far into the conversation, I called the president of the ministry organization she was raising support to join, and I asked what the policy was regarding someone working part-time to subsidize their needs. He seemed supportive as I shared that I grew up in a community where the ministers and youth workers in the church were also the mail clerk, a local teacher, a bank teller, and so on. The president then told me that his dad worked on cars while he pastored. So I proceeded to encourage this sister with the idea of wearing a volunteer tag two days a week and working the other three days in a different, paid role so she could take care of her bills. We both got excited as we continued the conversation about all of the possibilities of her ministering to those serving in the state juvenile facility.

The point is that despite the fact that it seemed obvious to me that this sister had every right to do what made the most sense—i.e.,

84

get a part-time job—there were the guidelines of the organization that had authority over us to consider. Observance and obedience.

THE ART OF LISTENING

Jesus had to develop through all of the same challenges as any other Jewish boy so that one day he could step into the position of someone who could sympathize with all of our afflictions and the things we go through in life. Hebrews 5:7-8 tells us, "In the days of His flesh, He offered up both prayers and supplications with loud crying and tears to the One able to save Him from death, and He was heard because of His piety. Although He was a Son, *He learned obedience from the things which He suffered*" (emphasis added, NASB).

In other words, Jesus learned obedience through the difficult things he faced in his life. Obedience was a choice even for Jesus— and he chose to submit because of his relationship with his heavenly Father. This should give great hope to those of us who struggle with obedience.

When, unbeknownst to his mother and father, Jesus stayed behind after the Passover in Jerusalem, he was learning how to listen to the voice of his heavenly Father more closely. As he told his mother when they returned for him at the temple, "Why did you seek Me? Did you not know that I must be about My Father's business?" (Luke 2:49, NKJV). The latter verse everybody knows and cites, but the next few verses are very important, too: "But they did not understand the statement which He spoke to them. Then He went down with them and came to Nazareth, and was subject to them, but His mother kept all these things in her heart" (Luke 2:50-51).

A lot of times when we hear God tell us what to do, we don't move forward because of fear. Of being misunderstood. Of being ridiculed. Of not fitting in. We tend to shy away. But Jesus didn't. He heard the voice of his father and obeyed. Here Jesus shows us in urban youth ministry—indeed, any ministry—how to do it: *There's no one on the planet like you. You were born with a specific purpose in God's mind. All of us get so caught up in fear of what people think that we fail to see the uniqueness of our own design. What is it that you felt like God sent you here to do? Stop following a systematic order and get on your faces. Don't stop dreaming. Don't lose your passion.* And even though his earthly parents didn't understand, Jesus left the temple with them and "was subject to them." Jesus, who needn't submit to anyone on earth, chose to submit to Mary and Joseph, and by doing so learned the benefits of obedience and humility.

Jesus shows us how he learned to obey and grow into his ministry, and it's the same process for us. The Father has prepared a place for us, like he prepared a place for Jesus; but unfortunately, a lot of times we believe we're supposed to arrive in the "place" of favor, blessing, and support because we feel called, or we saw a need and went of our own accord. But often that's not how it works. Again, Jesus went back with his parents and was willing to wait 18 years for his ministry to start. I believe the tendency for us is instead of walking day to day, watching God unfold what God wants to unfold in our lives, we want to build five urban ministries in next two years—we want the dynasty built *yesterday.* Ask yourself this question: *Have you prayed about where God is leading you? Are you getting ahead of yourself?* We have to listen to God's voice every step of the way.

What Did Jesus Demonstrate about Learning to Obey?

First we read about Jesus questioning his parents, asking them, "Why are you seeking Me?" It's important to realize that Jesus wasn't saying, "Don't you get it? I had to be up in here doing my father's business!" Rather, when he saw that they didn't understand, Jesus was willing to leave the temple and be obedient to them until the heavenly Father revealed to Mary and Joseph what he'd already revealed to Jesus. This is the difficult part—to trust God to bring change while we remain obedient to God's voice and learn to wait for others to gain an understanding of what we've seen and heard.

But often we can't hear what to do, especially when it comes to change, because we've become dull of hearing. Scientists who specialize in child development have followed the growth of the sense of hearing, learning that there are more than 50,000 neurons that connect the inner ear to the brain-hearing center. Although the human ear is designed to receive sounds, it doesn't actually "hear" them. After the ear receives the sound, the brain *translates* that sound into the *language of hearing.* Even though the ear picks up multiple sound bites every day, the brain actually chooses which ones to concentrate on and which ones to ignore.

For example, a man from a farm in upstate New York visits a friend at his Manhattan apartment. As they're walking down the crowded, noisy street, the friend from out of town thinks he hears a cricket in the bushes, and he tells his friend to listen. The man from the country thinks it's amazing that a cricket could survive the conditions of the crowded city. But the city friend laughs and asks him how in the world anyone could hear a cricket with all the noises of the city. The out-of-town friend looks at his city friend and says, "We hear what we're interested in hearing." He then takes a quarter out of his pocket and drops it on the sidewalk where it makes a clear, crisp ringing sound—and of course, everyone around them stops to see if they dropped the money.

In the same way, we listen to those with whom we have a relationship, and Jesus has a close relationship with his heavenly Father. This relationship developed throughout his life, as it should in ours. As we just learned, the brain has to evaluate and process all sounds, or else all sounds would be dealt with at the same level of importance. And listening extends into different aspects of communication—not all communication involves words alone.

Becoming Sensitive to Nuances

I continue to learn more about myself during this journey of urban youth ministry. And there are a few things I'm certain of—I have a passion for the disenfranchised, and I love to pour my life into those positioned in significant spheres of influence that affect the next generation (such as teachers and athletes and youth workers).

I grew up in a very passionate family and people group. But my passion also can result in misunderstandings and frustrations in others. When I'm passionate about empowering oppressed people, I tend to have little tolerance for those who don't understand that empowerment goes beyond giving somebody a job. Therefore, my tone of voice modulates; and more often than not, some people can misunderstand me and assume I'm angry. In the midst of those relational speed bumps, at times I didn't have the confidence in my heavenly Father's ability to speak into others' hearts what he was also revealing to me. Other times I needed to learn how to graciously say, "I disagree."

We all have nuances connected to the manner in which we communicate—and these nuances give observers the chance to size us up and test the authenticity of our intentions. Simply observing a group of people interact will tell us that each person is deciphering more than just spoken words. Tone, emphasis, pitch, posture, a touch, a smile, or a frown—all of these things contribute to deeper communication.

After the episode of the 12-year-old Jesus in the temple, he spent the next 18 years learning to hear with clarity the voice of God in the midst of a world of Jewish tradition and Roman oppression. We in urban youth ministry must also learn how to listen to God with same exacting quality and trust God's character when so many other sounds are clamoring to be heard.

Listening with Righteous Anger

The presence of poverty in Israel pervades the Gospels, a major cause being the Roman tax structure; there was also religious taxation that Jewish people rendered to the Jerusalem priestly hierarchy. The Roman colonization of Israel was the setting of Jesus' childhood. The suffering that the Romans visited on the Jewish people was so pervasive that it had to have an influence on Jesus' political consciousness and social life. The Bible tells us that, having become like man, Jesus understands the pains of humanity.

Yet Jesus also came in contact with the aristocratic, hereditary priestly class (Pharisees and Sadducees) that was the center of temple life. Because of their social standing and wealth, the Sadducees apparently wielded significant influence over the hereditary priests. In fact, some theologians believe the Sadducees' approach to religion was more materialistic than that of most first-century Jews. Meanwhile, the Pharisees lived for the "traditions of the fathers." They upheld and challenged everyone else to meet their standards of upholding rituals and laws.

The narrow-minded thinking of the Pharisees isn't far from where we are today in some of our ministerial thinking. We often see Christians taking a stand for godliness and justice, but only down the vein of a moral ideology while ignoring the economic exploitation of a class of people. Do we ask where all the money's going when it's sent to ministry corporate offices? Do we care who gets the tax break? Do we care that some ministries are simply building up a business on the back of religion? In the urban youth ministry landscape, are we building up a program that we want and ignoring the real needs all around us?

Wilderness Times—the Greatest
Places for Listening and Learning

Jesus dealt with Satan in the wilderness (Luke 4) using admonitions straight out of Deuteronomy. But Jesus didn't dialogue with Satan; he stated the truth to the enemy. I believe Jesus used the verses from Deuteronomy because his time of testing mirrored the time when the children of Israel were taken into the wilderness so that the Father God could humble them and test them to know what was in their hearts: "You shall remember all the ways which the Lord your God has led you in the wilderness these forty years, that He might humble you, testing you, to know what was in your heart, whether you would keep His commandments or not" (Deuteronomy 8:2, NASB).

The word used here for "testing" is the mining term, *smelting*. Smelting involves a great deal of heat to separate pure metal from a mixture of rock, ore, and other substances. Knowing that, it's easy to see the parallel with God wanting to use the time of the Israelites' desert wandering to get at the heart of what God created in the Israelites—because he'd already chosen them to be witnesses of God's reality to the whole world: "You are My witnesses," declares the Lord, "And My servant whom I have chosen, so that you may know and believe Me and understand that I am He. Before Me there was no God formed, and there will be none after Me" (Isaiah 43:10, NASB).

Further, Jesus was led into the wilderness by the Holy Spirit not for a time of testing (because God already knew what was in his Son) but for a time of *tempting*. As is typical of Satan, he messes with God's truth, giving lip service to part of it but not telling all of it. But Luke 4 tells us that Jesus rebuked the enemy with the lessons that had already been established in God's truth through the wilderness journey of the Israelites.

Just as Satan did during his first encounter with Eve—when he challenged her to question the meaning of what she'd been told about obedience to God's word—Satan challenged God's ability to provide by telling Jesus to turn stones into bread. But bread hadn't come from stones in the desert for the Israelites. When Moses struck a stone, it released water; the bread called "manna" had come down from heaven. Satan was speaking to the living Bread; and in a very real sense, he was asking Jesus, "Do you know who you are?" But Jesus wasn't led by his own flesh and ability; he was led by the Holy Spirit— and he was obedient to the voice of his Father's covenant character.

Jesus trusted that the journey of reconciliation and redemption had already taken place. "Who for the joy set before [Jesus] endured the cross" (Hebrews 12:2, NASB). Not the joy of the journey, not the joy of the tempting, not the joy of the cross, but the joy of the *results* of obedience, the joy of God's sons and daughters being established in right relationship with the Father forever. Hallelujiah!

Mentoring and Empowerment

In response to the declining test scores of graduates of America's public high schools, the government branch responsible for quality public education launched a movement to improve American schools (No Child Left Behind, 2002). This educational redesign program has focused on ways to improve student learning and performance, but it's also directed attention to the needs of teachers and how to empower them to provide more mastery of classroom learning opportunities.

A national survey group sampled teachers and asked them to share what they saw as their greatest needs for more effective teaching—and it was a school mentoring relationship with more experienced teachers. Mentoring was viewed as more valuable than both additional training in educational methods and strategies and extra college coursework. It seems that one of the reasons mentoring was rated as so valuable was because it had such a practical impact on teachers' daily lives. The most productive mentor relationship was with someone with more experience (more teaching years) and who was willing to meet on a weekly basis. The teachers shared that follow-through was critical to the relationship.

Jesus mentored his disciples, drawing strength to do so through his relationship with his heavenly Father. Jesus shared with his disciples in John 4 that doing the will of the Father even supplied him with bodily nourishment! In that same chapter, the disciples had gone into a Samaritan town to buy lunch while Jesus met with a woman who was a social outcast. At the end of their discourse, her eyes were opened to the fact that Jesus is the Messiah, her life was restored, and she became a spokeswoman for Christ to her community—and soon her community came to Jesus as well.

Is it possible that the example of the Samaritan woman at the well means that a mentoring relationship is most effective when it involves individuals from the same community, who, in obedience, agree to come together to strengthen the whole and glorify God? The Samaritan villagers knew this woman, and they didn't think very highly of her. But she was so dramatically impacted by this man named Jesus that they wanted to see him for themselves. In other words, the villagers weren't impressed by the disciples—they were impressed by a change in *one of their own*. It's a humbling and challenging thing to return to our own communities—the people who know our pasts and us. There's nowhere to hide; no masks we can put on to conceal our faults. But that knowledge of our pasts also allows our neighbors to witness the incredible change that takes place in our lives through the miraculous power of a risen Savior.

Also worth examining is the fact that Jesus didn't send his disciples into the Samaritan village to encourage the townspeople to come and meet with him. The Samaritan woman already had a relationship connection in her town—what she needed was a relationship with Jesus that she could then share.

Why do many urban youth ministry programs so often do everything backward? We encourage strangers to go into neighborhoods and talk to the people living in them about their needs when the *people living in these neighborhoods know these strangers haven't a clue about their real needs.* Why not involve individuals from the neighborhoods in ministry to the neighborhood? That way the trust relationship is developed more quickly and real-life needs can be attended to more realistically.

Jesus stayed in that village for two days to teach the people. I believe he also advised the elders of the village how to care for the other women in the town who were like the woman he met at the well, so they could grow in the new freedom of God's truth that they'd received from Jesus. I'm guessing he didn't leave them without a practical follow-up plan. Jesus didn't preach without interaction—he taught the truth in practical ways.

In urban youth ministry, we must do the same. We need to hear the needs of the people under our care. We have to look beyond the "big event" and develop follow-up plans. Sure, the board will get excited when we report a bunch of decisions for Christ. But now what are you going to do with those kids who made those decisions? Whatever directions we take, let them be in obedience to God.

DR. RENÉ'S PRESCRIPTION

for Accomplishing Obedience

- Master the art of listening—to God and to others
- Remember that obedience was a choice for Jesus, too
- Learn to love the virtue of patience (i.e., wait...and wait some more)
- Develop sensitivity to nuance
- Don't shrink back from wilderness experiences
- Champion mentor-mentee relationships within your community

Rx

QUESTIONS FOR DISCUSSION

1. Each urban community has its own fingerprint, which means each has specific needs, resources, talents, gifts, and styles of caring for its youth. Therefore every outreach program should begin with the collection of community data and a plan for implementation of your ministry outreach. When will you begin this endeavor?

2. What weaknesses in your program implementation are due to lack of practical information about community needs? How might more information about the community assist you in the development of your intervention plan to address youth and family needs?

3. How does your outreach minister to youth development? And how does your youth development encourage intellectual growth, increased social skills, and a healthier physical stature?

4. How isolated is your outreach program? Do you seek collaboration with other youth organizations?

5. What if a portion of each week was devoted to networking with other community outreaches? Don't be a stranger to the individuals you're serving with; gifts, talents, and resources can be increased exponentially by partnerships.

CHAPTER SIX

THE EFFECTIVENESS OF RITUALS AND RELATIONSHIPS
STRENGTHENED BY THE POWER OF BELIEF

I was a child of the civil rights era. Born in 1959, I believed some things about myself due to the voice of society and my new school community. My older sister, Karen, and I were the first children who looked like us to enter Ashfield Elementary School when we moved from the projects to Brockton, Massachusetts. And with the transition from Jim Crow in the 1950s, all the little black children were placed in "basic" classes—a remedial form of education back then.

I had no idea why we had to move from the projects to a neighborhood that didn't want us to begin with. The other children called my sister and me names (Karen was "Walking Tootsie Roll," and I was "Tootsie Roll Jr."), they pulled my pigtails, and they pushed me around until I began to fight back. Soon, I was fighting every day. And when I say "every day," I mean *every day*. You can ask my mother—she made appearances at the school office almost as much as I did. In fact my mother tells the story of how they sent a psychologist to the house to get me into a special class because I "obviously" had "some behavioral issues." (Sorry—I "obviously" didn't like being called names and being pushed around every day.)

Things got so bad that my fifth-grade teacher moved up with me to sixth grade. But prior to the move, she noticed that I was getting my work done quickly in the basic group, yet I was still getting into trouble. Turns out I'd finish my work before the little white boys and girls did, and this was not supposed to happen. The children who pushed me and called me a stupid n----r were conditioned by the generation before them and by their social community that black children (this was long before the term *African American* came into common usage) weren't supposed to be smarter than they were or have more than they did.

On the other end of the spectrum, some who lived in the projects thought my family members were a bunch of "Uncle Toms." (If they only knew.) We'd moved from the projects because my mother and stepfather had a sense of pride and a work ethic, and they saw the projects as a passing-through place for them. Then when my stepfather passed away, my mother—now widowed for the second time—was left with a house that required two incomes to cover the monthly payments. However, she refused to return to the projects. So we lived in a house, and she worked a job and received food stamps until she could get back on her feet, get into a nursing school, and move from LPN to RN status in order to increase her pay. She worked; we went to school—that was the deal. Emotionally, economically, and academically, it was a challenge.

One teacher—Miss Eagan—saw my academic potential, and she began to work at getting me moved up. Initially it didn't fly because the principal believed that "colored kids don't learn like our children do." But Miss Eagan was someone who walked the talk about community. Her persistence with my mother and with me eventually got me moved up to honors classes.

Then a sixth-grade coach saw some athletic potential in me. Slowly I developed a new belief system about myself. The focus became how fast I could run, how high I could jump, or how consistently I could shoot a ball through a circular iron goal—which wasn't a bad thing. It's just that, unfortunately, my belief system in regard to my academic potential didn't change until I became a Christian when I was a junior in college and began reading the Word of God for myself. Then I had to learn how to live out what I believed. Somehow God would move me from believing *I don't fit in with good students* to *I have the mind of Christ, and I can do all things through Christ who strengthens me.* This process is still ongoing—it's happening right now, in fact. (I never would've dreamed that I'd be Dr. anybody, but that's another story for another time.)

We all must go through processes. Me. You. Even the Israelites did this. After being enslaved for years and treated as less than human, they had much, much more to learn in the classroom of the desert.

BELIEF AFTER EGYPT

Evaluating the belief paradigms of the Israelites in the book of Exodus helps us to understand why they had trouble trusting a God they didn't know firsthand. This people group had been living in Egypt for 400 years (nearly the same duration as the Atlantic slave trade of West Africans), and their forebears' eyewitness encounters with God had long since become a grandparent's bedtime story. Such is the longevity of the storytelling cultures of the world. But while the stories kept God alive for the people, they didn't lead the people to experience a personal relationship with God.

The Israelites' belief system was influenced by their experiences in Egypt where they were subject to many authorities and gods. Ten generations of Israelites experienced their God's silence in the face of noisy Egyptian idolatry. They knew the unpredictable abuse and oppression practiced by slave masters who didn't care if they lived or died. Thus, the Israelites learned to be ruled by their needs of the moment. Daily needs are a luxury to a slave. Nourishment from food meant that they'd have enough strength to return from the work fields to their families, that their bodies could be empowered to fight off disease and illness, and that they could provide protection for their children. Just staying alive was a daily battle for this people group.

These experiences were the source of the long-term belief banks in the minds of the Israelites. Since beliefs are stored in our long-term memory, every piece of new information or learning must pass the test of what's already believed and stored in the brain. This bank of truth helps each individual make sense of events, understand natural laws, evaluate cause and effect, and develop decisions concerning goodness, truth, and beauty.

Long-term memories are used to interpret the world of relationships, too. Past experiences shape an individual's self-concept. For example, those who feel slighted by the greater society rarely feel good about themselves. The Israelites, slighted as they were by the Egyptians, saw wealthy Egyptians paying priests in an effort to secure their passage to eternal life, among other things. However, the poor in that day—as well as today—were more likely to be concerned with issues of daily survival as opposed to eternal questions.

But while God changed the Israelites' status from that of slaves to his "chosen people," what they'd already become convinced of in their minds didn't change. Could there be a similar belief bank in the minds of the urban poor of the world?

BELIEF AMONG CITY DWELLERS

Significant experiences have deep roots in the emotional areas of the brain. When an emotional event is very strong or has occurred multiple times, the brain marks that event as more important than other events and instructs the body to stay alert for the same event to occur again. When the brain identifies an emotionally significant event, that event has the potential to project the same emotions upon similar situations and relationships.

For example, an abusive relationship between a little girl and her father may cause the little girl to grow up expecting abusive relationships with every important male in her life. The cues from her past experiences inform her mental belief system that close male relationships may be abusive. Her interpretation of the abuse becomes an inevitable shaper of future relationships.

Often in urban ministry venues, individuals have experienced deep pains of rejection and abuse in the form of racism, classism, and sexism. I heard a sermon from a renowned preacher titled "The Leveling Place." In this message the speaker made the point that God makes all things equal at the leveling place of the Cross. He went on to discuss the fact that in the Bible we can see patterns of thinking that stayed with people for a generation before change occurred. For example, the children of Israel wandered in the wilderness for 40 years, thus allowing the "Egypt-minded" generation to die off so the next generation—who were raised in the wilderness (in other words, "the manna generation")—could testify to God's daily provision.

Science tells us that all learning can be relearned, unlearned, or replaced with new learning. Problems occur when old patterns of learning are reinforced by mental rehearsals of the past. This constant rehearsal allows those memory roots to be strengthened. And this dysfunctional way of thinking and acting can be detrimental to a person, no matter their social strata, gender, or ethnicity.

So what model is the brain designed to follow?

Genetic Potential

God designed the human brain for relationships. One of the first challenges that the Israelites faced in their first days of freedom from Egypt was a constant pull toward idolatry. *Idol* is defined in Webster's as "an object of extreme devotion." Still, idolatry is a type of relationship.

The television show *American Idol* is a singing competition that concludes with the naming of a winner who becomes an instant household name—and attracts the record-buying public with lots of CD sales. Idol worship in the Old Testament emanated from similar benign affections. Most ancient idols were personal statues of clay, metal, or wood, and they were used as good-luck charms. As "good luck" increased for the individual, so did the value of the idol.

Idol design was tied to the needs of the people. For example, if a farmer needed help, guidance, and blessings on his crops, or if a carpenter needed help with his skill or knowledge about how to market his products, he'd either adopt an idol that was already used by his profession, or he'd create a new one.

In ancient Ephesus, Diana was the goddess of fertility. Individuals sought her favor for bearing children, as well as reproductive favor with their livestock. When one community saw another community prosper, success wasn't attributed to the skills of the community members but to the power and influence of their idol gods.

Idolatry shows us that humans want a controllable image. God removed the Israelites from a land of idolatry to show them that he was the God of the land. "You yourselves have seen what I did to the Egyptians, and how I bore you on eagles' wings and brought you to Myself" (Exodus 19:4, NASB).

The Evolution of a Covenant Relationship

The first time the word *covenant* is used in the Bible is in the story of Noah. God told Noah that he would establish a covenant with Noah and his sons and that the flood that was going to cover the earth wouldn't destroy them. The next time we see the word *covenant* is when God is making a covenant with Abraham's seed. This is especially interesting since Abraham doesn't have any children at this point—his wife, Sarah, is barren. Therefore, God had to provide all of the necessary aspects and conditions of the Abrahamic covenant relationship. God was going to awaken the world that had been birthed

100

into death in the garden of Eden, just by the power of the seed of his Word. What a promise!

The covenant covering moved from Abraham to his son Isaac to his grandson Jacob and to Jacob's 12 sons, who eventually populated the nation of Israel. One of the sons, Abraham's great-grandson Joseph, would then bring the "seed" of Abraham into a relationship with Egypt for the price of grain to feed the other 11 tribes. These 12 tribes originally entered Egypt as guests. But after the death of Joseph, their relationship with Pharaoh changed to that of slaves, and the 12 tribes remained in Egypt for 400 years, multiplying from a people group of about 70 to more than a million by the time God brought them out of bondage.

The covenant relationship God established with the Israelites was only in seed form with Abraham, but it continued to grow throughout the centuries. In the same way, God's Word is living so that what is begun by God grows—just as it was in the beginning when God spoke life into the planet earth and it began to bring forth what was spoken into it.

The original covenant was between the reproductive portion of Abraham and his wife Sarah, which was symbolic of the reproductive portion of God's Word being deposited into a womb that would bring forth worshipers and witnesses to testify who God is to the nations of the world.

Isaiah shares in 43:10 that the Israelites were chosen by God to be his witnesses and servants so they might know and believe that God is who he proclaims himself to be:

"You are my witnesses," declares the Lord, "and my servant whom I have chosen, so that you may know and believe me and understand that I am he. Before me no god was formed, nor will there be one after me."

The covenant also carried with it the presupposition of a relationship, and the Israelites were then placed in training over the next 40
years in the desert.

Promotion of Relationship Through Rituals

In Genesis, the triune God spoke of making the human species in God's
own image. The only portion of creation that was not called "good"
was the fact that the first human was alone. This appears to indicate
that humans are designed to need community and relationships.

When the Israelites moved out of Egypt and began their desert
wandering, God designed the tabernacle so that each religious ritual
was done in community with other believers. And one of the points
of being part of a community was that it helped the believers live
out their beliefs. It was also a visual and physical expression of God's
redemptive work in their lives. The organization and building of the
tabernacle was so important that 50 chapters in the Bible are devoted
to a description of it and its ministries, compared to only two chapters devoted to a description of creation.

The tabernacle paints a picture of a God of order who is holy
yet full of grace, mercy, and love. In the season of desert living, the
tabernacle was literally at the center of community life, with all 12
tribes camped around it. Later, the temple functioned as a focal point
of Israel's community life. God used the language of the services and
feasts of the tabernacle to teach the people how to know and love
him. The tabernacle and temple were organized to communicate in a
language that the people had been divinely created to understand. It
makes no sense to give someone a book written in a language they've
never encountered before—but if they're given a key to translate the
book, the reading of the book can be purposeful.

Communication Through Rituals

As outlined in Sousa's *How the Brain Works*, his research uncovered the presence of "mirror neurons" in the brain. Their function is to fire when a person observes actions performed by someone else. The neurons then "mirror" the behavior of others, as though the observer were doing the acting.

God is a master communicator. God allowed every aspect of the construction of the tabernacle to have meaning and significance to the people. The tabernacle was a brilliant simulation of what Christ would perform for all people thousands of years later, and the Israelites were given the opportunity, in a sense, to experience Christ. The tabernacle was designed to change the brains of the Israelites and the way they thought about God.

Many of the events surrounding the Israelites' exodus from Egypt carried a strong emotional impact. The drama of the plagues, the night the Israelites readied themselves to leave, putting lamb's blood on their doorposts, the quick cooking of the lamb, making bread without yeast because there'd be no time for it to rise—everything was designed to allow them to flee. God established the celebration of the Passover so the Israelites would continue to remember and celebrate how God rescued them from captivity.

The tabernacle was designed to speak to all five senses and cater to different individual learning styles. Every act was personalized—personal sacrifices were presented to the priests, and the head of each family had to present the animal and lay hands on its head before it was killed. Each family was tutored through their "walk" in the tabernacle by a priest who served them by washing in the bronze laver, repeating the word of God's promises, burning the incense, and sprinkling the blood sacrifice on the mercy seat. The people experienced worship in the presence of prayer and community relationships.

Learning Principles
Extensive research concerning the retention of learning indicates that

70 to 90 percent of all new learning is lost in the first 18 to 24 hours after it's taught. The tabernacle, however, allowed a repetition of the lessons so that information became a living part of each individual. The synergistic piece of each tribe having its own part to perform was a way to multiply the aspect of community learning and involvement. Each tribe was given a separate duty that only the members of that tribe could perform, and that duty was then passed down to the next generations.

The rituals provided the Israelites with a remembrance of their past and a record of who they were to God. The rituals functioned as a continual walking history tour, allowing individuals to draw on the past experience of God's hand in their lives, as well as the predictive power of how God would participate and respond in their future. God is the designer of all things, and God knows how he created us to think.

I believe that we must begin to recognize that you and I are of "another culture" and people group when we become Christians—and in this way, we are united. Our citizenship is in heaven, not of this earth. God will prepare us in whatsoever way he chooses for whatever he has in store for us.

Because of the journey the Father has designed for me, I've been able to minister in almost any venue you can imagine. God is more than able. Therefore, we in urban youth ministry must keep in mind that we'll be sent wherever God chooses, whenever God chooses, and to whomever God chooses. The challenge for us is to have the mind of Christ and not cling to our old opinions of things.

If we truly embrace the concept that we are united in Christ, then the rest will naturally fall into place. I've shared the U.N.I.T.Y. acronym all over the United States, as well as in South Africa, and I believe it to be true. May it help you in your process as well.

U: United in Christ

N: New Paradigm of Thinking. Once you know that you are first and foremost a child of God, born from above, you have to take time to study the Scriptures about your new nature. What does it mean to be a child of God?

I: Individual Expressions of God's Glory. This is the beauty of diversity. When we truly begin to appreciate who God created us to be as born-again African-American women, or born-again Native-American men, or born-again Latino children, or born-again Caucasian teenagers, or any other color or age group—whatever the external vessel that the Spirit of God is housed in shall become only the container from which the Spirit of God is poured out. Let's learn to respect the people God has individually made us to be.

T: Teachable. This one is difficult for most individuals because once we've been raised a certain way, we usually fight change. However, the nature of God's kingdom is what should be pouring forth from our natural vessels. But here's the real sticking point: The only way the light of God's nature can truly pour out of us is if our outer shells are broken! We're called to die to our old ways of doing things so the nature of Christ can shine through us. This is what Paul refers to in 2 Corinthians 5:17—"If anyone is in Christ, the new creation has come: The old has gone, the new is here!" Will you allow the Spirit of God to teach you what you need to know about working and serving in a new community?

Y: Yield to the Holy Spirit's Leading, Not Your Old Paradigm of Culture. This is when the power of God is allowed to take over. Every time we choose to walk in a kingdom perspective above our culture and ethnicity and to respect and honor those of other cultures (esteem your brother or sister as more important than yourself), God is ultimately glorified. This is the challenge to all of us, to walk in this kind of nature!

I close this section with Paul's words to the people at the church in Philippi.

> If you've gotten anything at all out of following Christ, if his love has made any difference in your life, if being in a community of the Spirit means anything to you, if you have a heart, if you care—then do me a favor: Agree with each other, love each other, be deep-spirited friends. Don't push your way to the front; don't sweet-talk your way to the top. Put yourself aside, and help others get ahead. Don't be obsessed with getting your own advantage. Forget yourselves long enough to lend a helping hand. Think of yourselves the way Christ Jesus thought of himself. He had equal status with God but didn't think so much of himself that he had to cling to the advantages of that status no matter what. Not at all. When the time came, he set aside the privileges of deity and took on the status [culture] of a slave, became human! Having become human, he stayed human. It was an incredibly humbling process. He didn't claim special privileges. Instead, he lived a selfless, obedient life and then died a selfless, obedient death—and the worst kind of death at that—a crucifixion. (Philippians 2:1-8, *The Message*)

So you and I, in order to walk as Jesus walked, must allow our beliefs to change us. We must be willing to die to ourselves and to esteem our brothers and sisters as more important, allowing for the peace and harmony that God intended. Can we learn from one another and grow together in unity and harmony? This is crucial if we're going to fight for one another and go into battle together against a strong enemy for the sake of youth in the urban landscape. This is how we'll fight the good fight of faith!

DR. RENÉ'S PRESCRIPTION
for Increasing the Power of Belief through Effective Relationships and Rituals

- Understand that long-held beliefs can take a long time to change
- Recognize idolatry in its many forms (and avoid it)
- Seek to establish convenant-based relationships
- Identify and utilize positive symbols and rituals from your community
- Always strive for unity and harmony

QUESTIONS FOR DISCUSSION

1. Romans 12 states that our minds are transformed in the process of being renewed. An unrenewed mind is in danger of being conformed to the thinking patterns of the world. *How do you allow your mind to be renewed on a consistent basis?*

2. Many youth today lack a sense of identity and are looking for it in all the wrong places. God thought it was important to tell the children of Israel that they were children of *promise.* Is it possible that the children of Israel were just as confused as the youth of today? Could this be why the children of Israel needed their true identity spoken into their lives? Discuss ways you can work with the youth of your community and encourage them to understand their purpose and promised identity.

3. Only God can change hearts. Our ministries can plant and water, but it is the Lord who causes growth in the lives of our youth and their families. Being assured of this truth helps us rest in our assigned mission. Read Matthew 11:28-29 and ask yourself this question: *How heavy is my load, and where do I need to rest more?* If you have difficulty resting, find out why.

4. *Don't allow your own grace to be buried.* This is a powerful directive that many of us in urban youth ministry struggle with. We're often tempted to live a life of performance that a board will endorse after we bring results. When we don't see visible signs of our ministry efforts producing changed lives, we can respond with negativity and self-condemning attitudes, lacking the faith that God is using us. Having an attitude of grace allows us to keep the Lord as the initiator and sustainer of change. *In what ways have you felt unproductive, dissatisfied, or inadequate? Where does the principle of grace minister to you in these areas?*

5. All of us are like cracked pots, but God has good news for cracked pots: We were broken vessels of clay, restored by the Master Potter and Craftsman. Our areas of weakness don't surprise God, and God is able to heal our brokenness. Write down the areas of your life that you believe are still in the process of healing. We're designed to walk in fellowship with other believers: Are you in a trust-based relationship with someone who allows you room to be honest about hindrances to your spiritual growth and development? If there is no one, pray that God will reveal to you who that person should be.

CHAPTER SEVEN

MODELS OF INTERCESSION
WHO HAS YOUR BACK?

"I looked for someone among them who would build up the wall and stand before me in the gap on behalf of the land so I would not have to destroy it, but I found no one" (Ezekiel 22:30). This passage of Ezekiel refers to the moral decay of the city. The prophet was speaking God's words to the city's leadership and using the breached wall as an example. He's saying that if the enemies of the city had attacked and penetrated the wall, then the Israelites would do whatever was necessary to fill in the gap and mend the breach. However, in this case the enemies aren't outside; the corruption is within the city walls—beginning with the city's leaders. Within the four classes of leadership—princes, priests, officials, and prophets—no one could be found to repair the moral damage that had been done to the nation.

The passage in Ezekiel still speaks to us today, as we know of only one Man who stood in the gap for all human beings in order to repair the breach of sin—Jesus Christ. He's the Prince of Peace and our great High Priest who officiated kingdom business and spoke the prophetic words of God. Jesus knew the Law as a little boy and teenager. He grew up learning about the prophets of Ezekiel's time and in a community where he had an opportunity to witness the corruption of humanity. (Later in the chapter we'll deal with corruption in local leadership.)

In Jesus' day it was customary for the fathers and the religious leaders of the community to teach and model prayer and intercession for the next generation. And since the sinful nature of the world separates human beings from God, we're all in need of an intercessor. In the following pages, we'll take a look at what was modeled to Jesus about the intercessory prayers of a leader.

As would happen during the early years of any young Jewish boy's life, Jesus became familiar with the writings of Moses, as well as Moses' leadership style. Moses was seen as an intercessory leader: "Therefore He said that He would destroy them, had not Moses His chosen one stood before Him in the breach, to turn away His wrath, lest He destroy *them*" (Psalm 106:23, NKJV).

Moses' writings offer more details about this incident:

Then Moses pleaded with the Lord his God, and said: "Lord, why does Your wrath burn hot against Your people whom You have brought out of the land of Egypt with great power and with a mighty hand? Why should the Egyptians speak, and say, 'He brought them out to harm them, to kill them in the mountains, and to consume them from the face of the earth'? Turn from Your fierce wrath, and relent from this harm to Your people. Remember Abraham, Isaac, and Israel, Your servants, to whom You swore by Your own self, and said to them, 'I will multiply your descendents as the stars of heaven; and all this land that I have spoken of I give to your descendents, and they shall inherit *it* forever.'" So the Lord relented from the harm which He said He would do to His people. (Exodus 32:11-14, NKJV)

This image represents the intercession that can take place between the people and God.

LESSONS IN PRAYER

Throughout the Gospels it's likely that much of what the disciples learned was "caught" (rather than formally "taught") by simply being in the presence of Jesus. The synoptic Gospel of Luke records the statement: "Lord, teach us to pray" (11:1). The *Jesus* film, produced by Campus Crusade for Christ, shows Peter approaching Jesus and making the same request. The scene also alludes to the fact that Peter witnessed what happened in Jesus' life as a result of Jesus being in the presence of God through prayer.

So where did Jesus learn how to pray? Prayer was of primary importance in Jewish life. It was a daily obligation and a positive precept taken from the Torah, which commands the people to serve God every day: "So you shall serve the Lord your God" (Exodus 23:25, NKJV) and "Fear the Lord your God, serve him only and take your oaths in his name" (Deuteronomy 6:13).

The Hebrew word for prayer, *tefillah*, comes from the Hebrew verb meaning "to supplicate or to judge." When Jesus told his disciples to *tefillah*, or pray, "Our Father which art in heaven, hallowed be thy name" (Matthew 6:9, KJV), he was making a radical point. Jesus grew up learning that through prayer we judge ourselves; through the introspection of prayer, we can raise our standard of moral conduct as we strive to be like God and fulfill our potential as human beings. But as the coming Messiah, Jesus spoke of prayer as a way for us to witness our God and Father establishing his kingdom in our lives and throughout the earth—a totally different approach and viewpoint.

In other words, our introspection and self-discipline don't make us more like God or lead us to self-improvement in the eyes of God. Rather, the Scriptures tell us that before time began, God foreknew us and planned that we'd be conformed to the image of his Son— brought in tune with what God is doing. And prayer is the vehicle through which we're transformed. Through life's experiences we learn to cry out to God, and during times of difficulty we learn about the God who cares for us and is committed to working out of us whatever hinders us from becoming more like his Son (Romans 8:29).

In Jesus' day, the *tefillah* was more than simply pleading with God; it provided worshipers the opportunity to proclaim their Jewish identity within the community and to perpetuate the holy language of Hebrew. Jesus told his disciples they wouldn't be left as orphans without an identity or inheritance, but they'd be given the promised Holy Spirit that would seal their hearts and be with them and in them forever (see John 14:16-18). Paul told the Christians at Ephesus that because of their trust in Christ—in whom they had believed after hearing the Word of truth and the gospel of their salvation—they'd be sealed with the Holy Spirit of promise who is the guarantee of their inheritance (see Ephesians 1:13-14). Access to God and God's kingdom doesn't come through earthly pedigree, ethnicity, or culture, but through the bloodline of Christ our Lord. As adopted children of God, we've all been granted entrance to the throne room of grace "so that we may receive mercy and find grace to help us in our time of need" (Hebrews 4:16).

A question that's been on the table for the last two decades of urban youth ministry is this: *Why do so many men and women who were raised in the inner cities of our nation and born again into God's kingdom have the propensity to look to other cultures or people groups to "rescue" the youth of their own communities?* Since God allowed these urban brothers and sisters to live and learn in those very communities—just as Jesus lived and learned in Nazareth— doesn't it make sense that one day they would be appointed and anointed to restore the breached walls of their own cities?

PREPARED TO STAND IN THE GAP

It was January of 1981. I'd been a Christian for about nine months, and some friends who were affiliated with Campus Crusade for Christ invited me to attend a conference titled "Chicago '81." This conference was significant in that it was designed and run by African Americans who were submitting to the call of Christ on their campuses. I still remember the keynote speakers: Crawford Loritts, Haman Cross Jr. and his mother (who many called "Mother Cross"), Tom Fritz, and the late Dr. E. V. Hill. As I reflect on that time, I'm amazed how all the messages are coming back to mind. Three of the messages I still speak of to this day.

The opening word was from Dr. Hill. I can still hear his voice when he shared the phrase, "Get up off your knees—all you do is pray, sing, and shout!" He told us this was the title of the cover story of a 1968 issue of Ebony magazine that addressed the "church negro" who really wasn't getting anything done by praying, singing, and shouting in the midst of a civil-rights crisis.

Haman Cross Jr. spoke about Christians being "a peg in a holy place"—being a set-apart people for a divine purpose planned by God before time began. And Mother Cross challenged many of us to "push away from the table" and become spiritually fat. She challenged us to feed on God in order to feed others.

But Dr. Hill's keynote address—"Up Off Our Knees!"—was the most memorable for me. The crowd was stirred as he took that article title and built a powerful exhortation. The premise he established was that many in the '60s believed that spiritual African Americans weren't getting things done by just praying, singing, and shouting. Then he took us on a historical journey of all that had transpired while we were "just" praying, singing, and shouting. We built Spelman College by just praying, singing, and shouting; we built Tuskegee University by just praying, singing, and shouting; we built Howard University by just praying, singing, and shouting; we sent the first African American to congress by just praying, singing, and shouting; we built Atlanta Mutual (now Atlanta Life Financial Group) by just praying, singing, and shouting. And he continued adding to this list for about three minutes.

To build his case, Dr. Hill shared how a spiritual people who cared about their own continued to make great strides as they pressed their way forward in prayer, invoking the God of the universe to make a way for those whom he had called for such a time as this. Hill's message continued to crescendo as people rose to their feet.

Then Dr. Hill calmed the crowd when he said, "Can I tell you what has happened since we've been up off our knees? Over half of our historically black colleges have closed, up off our knees. Drugs have infiltrated our communities, up off our knees. Gang violence is on the rise, up off our knees. Black-on-black crime is at an all-time high, up off our knees...." And the list went on as he challenged the African-American college population to *get back on our knees again* for the future of our communities. I can remember the somberness of the room at that moment.

That evening a mass of African-American college students began to kneel, stand, and lay prostrate before God, crying out for our communities. We took God at his Word: "If My people who are called by My name will humble themselves, and pray and seek My face, and turn from their wicked ways, then I will hear from heaven, and will forgive their sin and heal their land" (2 Chronicles 7:14, NKJV).

I'll never forget those few days in Chicago. Afterward, numerous people who'd attended the conference began to move out and do what God had spoken to all of our hearts. At the University of Texas, I started an organization called Black Christians on Campus. For years there had been Christian ministries on campus, but they were 99 percent Caucasian—and none of them were reaching the minority student population. We had our first event in the UT ballroom, and many students attended. As this particular event began to grow, a campus movement to reach out to the minority students was started. We didn't focus on salvation alone, but we walked out the definition of evangelism—sharing the "good news" of God's kingdom. In other words, we weren't just talking about heaven and hell. That's part of the good news, but it's not *all* of the good news. For many of the minority students on campus, they needed to hear about God meeting their needs today—getting school loans, having money to buy food, finding that important part-time job, etc.

Still, our main concern was the spiritual growth and development of young people. We talked about walking as a young man or woman of God when faced with some of the difficulties of being a minority student in the classroom, as well as on an athletic team. We talked a lot about standing up for Christ and how to share the salvation message. But many students lacked Bible knowledge that could inform them about subjects such as overcoming rejection, prejudice, and addictive behavior patterns. So we addressed generational strongholds (i.e., thought patterns) and also how to walk in true forgiveness. We taught them the basic foundations of the faith and how it applied to our lives as students on the UT campus. Thus the movement began.

We also started a small Bible study that met in the Jester East lounge. Each week it grew by word of mouth alone. After a few years, we moved from the lounge to a lecture hall in the University Teaching Center (UTC) building. By 1990, we were more than 100 strong in the lecture hall. If you didn't get there early, then you didn't get a seat. The room was filled with students from every walk of life. We had Latino, African American, White, and Asian students from three different campuses—Baylor, Southwest Texas State University, and Southwestern University in Georgetown—coming on a regular basis to hear the Word of God. Even some high school students started coming. I still look back in awe at what God did.

While I was doing what the Father had laid on my heart, the Chicago '81 conference had grown into the Impact Movement—a conference held every other year designed to minister and encourage

African-American students on campuses around the country. What a mighty God we serve! The message of God's kingdom will not be stopped. Men and women of color who are serious about reaching their communities with a holistic message of the gospel are still being raised up.

But Where Are They?

So if all of these young men and women are being raised up—where are they? The beginning of this chapter focuses on the biblical standard of raising up leaders from among the people.

Remember that when Ezekiel talked about the moral decay of the city, he was addressing the leadership—and the breached wall was his example. The enemies aren't waiting to attack from outside the city. The real problems are often within the city's walls—beginning with its leaders.

For years the challenge in every culture has been leadership development. Who's investing in the future leaders of urban America or even the urban centers around the world? When I think back to the young people who attended Chicago '81 as college students, we're all about 40 to 50 years old now. *Where are the thriving leaders from among our children's generation? Why aren't they readying themselves for ministry or already serving somewhere? Are they out there? What are they doing? What's happened? Is God moving in the inner cities of our country?*

I believe God is moving, but we fail to see God do so because we're blinded by our personal perceptions of what urban ministry "should be." There are many young people with hearts to minister to the needs of their peers in their communities, so they decided to get degrees and go back into the city to teach our young children how to read, write, and do functional mathematics. For many new college graduates, this seemed more attractive than joining a suburban ministry that felt called to become more diverse and planned to reach the youth of urban America. In the early nineties, very few ministries had an understanding of holistic outreach, but now it's "the thing" to have a holistic ministry.

When I finished my dissertation in 1999, I'd designed a holistic ministry model built by listening for more than a decade to the men and women who'd been speaking to this issue. For example, Dr. James Tyms—like the late Paulo Freire—believed that a true sense of community depends upon and is rooted in a God-conscious concern that's shared by those who make up the community. This is where those called to reach the next generation must be willing to cry out to God—to intercede—for the next generation. An awakened consciousness comes only from the Father above. According to Dr. Tyms, a true sense of community is grounded in a people's awakened consciousness of the nature and function of the church in a changing society— and rooted in the quality of relationships nurtured into existence and sustained by those who will be creative participants in the affairs of the community.

That said, if a community of believers from both the local church as well as parachurch organizations will organize its resources effectively into a united force, it would be better able to minister to the needs of the urban community.

MODELING INTERCESSION

For years many African-American theologians felt the pressing need to nurture the community through the vehicle of the church. The emphasis, they said, must be on addressing the need for a church curriculum that's relevant to the group it's attempting to reach and teach. Where I see similarities today to the type of leadership Ezekiel addressed in regard to the breached wall is with men and women taking bits and pieces of what's "relevant" to the next generation, preaching it from the pulpit, and stirring the hearts and minds of young people. But there's a lack of training once the concept has been introduced. It's as though they're performing surgery, closing up the wound, and not offering any follow-up care. Healing is a process, and ongoing nurturing is essential for broken and wounded places to be fully restored.

That's where we in urban youth ministry come in.

Dr. Norma Cook Everist, in her book *The Church as a Learning Community*, talks about people learning from one another by being models and mentors. She writes that for years the church emphasized that adults were to be good examples for the young people. She then takes note of the legalism many churches experience as a result of attempting to produce people who act in certain socially acceptable ways. This can result in shortcomings and hypocrisy, which typically leads to feelings of disillusionment and disappointment with Christianity.

A state of disillusionment is where much of urban ministry is today. There are numerous groups attempting cross-cultural urban outreach. But the continued challenge is to build community-based collaborative efforts. This can take place only when we're willing to let go of our own perceptions of urban ministry and learn from those who may have some insights that we're unaware of.

Teaching urban youth to follow Christ is not a packaged program. There are risks involved, but it can be very exciting when we're willing to launch out beyond our comfort zones. This is an ongoing journey that can be messy. Jesus told the first four disciples, who all happened to come from the same community, that he was about to make them "fishers of men" (Matthew 4:18-22; Mark 1:16-20). Christ didn't negate their gifts and talents; instead he met each disciple where they were. There would come a time for these disciples to be launched into the foreign territory of cross-cultural ministry. But first each of them had to learn the basics of the faith and have an opportunity for the Word of God to be fleshed out among them as they walked with Jesus.

The leaders of Ezekiel's day didn't model a willingness to stand in the gap for the needs of the people. The prophets, priests, city officials, and others weren't looking at the issues honestly. Instead, they were—as noted by Rick Renner, a preacher I heard many times in Austin—merchandising their anointing. Today we see this as a blab-it-and-grab-it mentality of confession rather than a corporate crying out to God for the needs of the community. We, therefore, must be careful of those who're "talking a good game" or peddling the gospel. Instead we're to be the vessels through which divine favor can flow to those who need it most. To those dealing with misfortune in their lives. In our youth ministries, that means instead of throwing money at a problem and praying it will go away, we instead come along-side youth and teach them to cope with pressures—even how to cry out to God when their hearts are a mess.

If we'd come back to the place of corporate prayer, praise, and worship and place our youth in the hands of the Holy Spirit as we teach and instruct them, then the young people will grow as God sees fit. And we'll end up being role models without even knowing it. The mentor piece is a matter of mutual respect, admiration, and consent.

Hang Up Your Superhero Cape

Dr. Everist speaks to one of the places that leads to danger for many—desiring to be the hero or the one upon whom another depends. She states, "Admiration can invite us to live only in the shadow of another. Mentors do well to guard against the ego satisfactions of keeping someone dependent." (*The Church as a Learning Comunnity*, 109)

Can we be content with these relationships growing into friend-ships? Into true peer relationships? I hope so. Jesus told his disciples, "I no longer call you servants, because servants do not know their master's business. Instead, I have called you friends, for everything that I learned from my Father I have made known to you" (John 15:15). We must do the same. In urban youth ministry, we need to pour our lives into kids—in the hope that they'll grow in their relationships with Christ and mature to peer relationships with former mentors. But we must also seek out brothers and sisters to mentor us, to pour their lives into us. Both endeavors are indispensable.

DR. RENÉ'S PRESCRIPTION
for Accomplishing Deep Intercession

- Recognize the importance—and harness the power—of prayer
- Don't forget that intercession isn't always done on your knees
- Meet others' physical needs with as much passion as their spiritual needs
- Don't miss the opportunity to lift up the future leaders of the community
- Be willing to "come alongside" and be a vessel through which divine favor flows
- Hang up your superhero cape
- Make it your goal to see those you mentor become your equals

QUESTIONS FOR DISCUSSION

In my years of urban ministry, I've witnessed many individuals (and at times myself) toiling over raising money, building projects, and planning massive outreach campaigns—and becoming worn down by the struggle. But Jesus tells us to come to him when we are weary, heavy-laden, and overburdened, and he will give us rest. We must return to the place of prayer and trust that God will fulfill the needs of the community as we continue to cry out to him and walk out our predestined purposes in the community. After all, God doesn't need our help. And when we don't believe God will come through, there's a tendency to pervert the blessings of the Lord and prostitute the principle of God's provision by emotionally manipulating others through devices such as sad stories and photographs. So we put on the event, raise the building, and hire the new charismatic individual who can, in our minds, "reach the masses." Six months after the event, the building, and hiring, we wonder why there's no productivity and multiplication. I'm beginning to understand that there's no conception where there's been no intimacy. Therefore we must return to the bedroom chambers of the Lord in prayer and know that it's God's nature and desire to move in the hearts and minds of all the people for whom we're interceding.

1. Take some time to write out the prayer that Jesus taught the disciples to pray (i.e., the Lord's Prayer: Matthew 6:9-13). What does this prayer teach us about the will of God for the city (see v. 10)?

2. When Jesus said to go into your room and pray (Matthew 6:6), he literally meant our bedroom chambers. This is where you share intimate things with that intimate one in your life—your spouse. But in our relationship with God, we—all of us—are the bride of Christ. Therefore pour out your heart to the Lord for the community that desperately needs change. Write down on a sheet of paper all the things you know are needed in the lives of the people of your community (note: not things you need for the ministry). Once your list is complete, begin praying

about those things, asking for God's kingdom to come into all the areas on your list.

3. The following is an exercise to encourage you in your time of prayer; take some time to answer these questions:

> a. Do you have a place that's comfortable, peaceful, and available in which to pray?
>
> b. Ask the Lord for grace to discipline your body to sit still in prayer for an extended period of time. Start somewhere: 10 minutes, 20 minutes, whatever suits you. (Although Jesus asked the disciples why they couldn't pray with him for an hour!)
>
> c. Is your prayer conversational, or are you doing all the talking? (Train your ear to listen and hear.)
>
> d. Do you have a format for prayer? The model in Matthew 6:9-13 is a great one.

CHAPTER EIGHT

NATIONS IN THE NEIGHBORHOOD

Have you ever gone into a store to check out a product you saw in a magazine or newspaper? What was the actual product like? Did it meet your expectations? Were the specifications of the product true to the description in the store's ad? Unfortunately, when we view something in a store, we sometimes find it isn't what we expected.

While visiting with numerous youth workers over the last 20 years, I've found that we all have our own perceptions of what constitutes "diverse ministry." The danger of an individual perception is that it has the potential to set the standard of ministry structure for diversity. We must be careful that ministry isn't built on the foundation of one man or one woman's experience (good or bad); instead the foundation must always be the truth of God's Word. The psalmist tells us "Unless the Lord builds the house, they labor in vain who build it" (Psalm 127:1, NASB).

Business concepts and research theory encourage us to have a blueprint of a replicable model. In the same way, I've sat in numerous meetings and heard conversations about the need for a "diversity ministry model": *What should the model look like? Should a northern inner-city model differ from a southern inner-city model?* "God only knows" is probably the best answer. Indeed, that's where we need to begin: To let the Creator of the universe set the standard of diversity in urban youth ministry.

THE NECESSITY OF MODELS

Did Jesus have a rationale for telling his disciples during their first year of ministry: "Do not enter a city of the Samaritans. But go rather to the lost sheep of the house of Israel" (Matthew 10:5-6, NKJV)? This question will be investigated with a probable hypothesis: *Jesus waited until he'd had a few years to minister to his disciples, allowing them time to deal with cultural biases and prejudice.* It wasn't until after Jesus had ascended that the Holy Spirit gave the disciples permission to go into Samaria and other Gentile nations. Peter still had issues with the Gentiles long after Jesus' ascension, illustrating the lengthy and sometimes difficult process of a mind in renewal.

After the day of Pentecost, the Holy Spirit became Peter's tutor and mentor. Jesus had told the disciples that he would send the Holy Spirit "to teach you all things, and bring to your remembrance all things that I said to you" (John 14:26). The Spirit of God would now have to bring to Peter's remembrance all that Jesus had taught and modeled before the disciples in regard to diversity and equality. And the Spirit got through. Check out how it happened in Acts 10:9-35, 44-48:

> About noon the following day as they were on their journey and approaching the city, Peter went up on the roof to pray. He became hungry and wanted something to eat, and while the meal was being prepared, he fell into a trance. He saw heaven opened and something like a large sheet being let down to earth by its four corners. It contained all kinds of four-footed animals, as well as reptiles and birds. Then a voice told him, "Get up, Peter. Kill and eat."
>
> "Surely not, Lord!" Peter replied. "I have never eaten anything impure or unclean."
>
> The voice spoke to him a second time, "Do not call anything impure that God has made clean."

This happened three times, and immediately the sheet was taken back to heaven.

While Peter was wondering about the meaning of the vision, the men sent by Cornelius found out where Simon's house was and stopped at the gate. They called out, asking if Simon who was known as Peter was staying there.

While Peter was still thinking about the vision, the Spirit said to him, "Simon, three men are looking for you. So get up and go downstairs. Do not hesitate to go with them, for I have sent them."

Peter went down and said to the men, "I'm the one you're looking for. Why have you come?"

The men replied, "We have come from Cornelius the centurion. He is a righteous and God-fearing man, who is respected by all the Jewish people. A holy angel told him to ask you to come to his house so that he could hear what you have to say." Then Peter invited the men into the house to be his guests.

The next day Peter started out with them, and some of the believers from Joppa went along. The following day he arrived in Caesarea. Cornelius was expecting them and had called together his relatives and close friends. As Peter entered the house, Cornelius met him and fell at his feet in reverence. But Peter made him get up. "Stand up," he said, "I am only human myself."

While talking with him, Peter went inside and found a large gathering of people. He said to them: "You are well aware that it is against our law for a Jew to associate with Gentiles or visit them. But God has shown me that I should not call anyone impure or unclean. So when I was sent for, I came without raising any objection. May I ask why you sent for me?"

Cornelius answered: "Three days ago I was in my house praying at this hour, at three in the afternoon. Suddenly a man in shining clothes stood before me and said, 'Cornelius, God has heard your prayer and remembered your gifts to the poor. Send to Joppa for Simon who is called Peter. He is a guest in the home of Simon the tanner, who lives by the sea.' I sent for you immediately, and it was good of you to come. Now we are all here in the presence of God to listen to everything the Lord has commanded you to tell us."

Then Peter began to speak: "I now realize how true it is that God does not show favoritism but accepts those from every nation who fear him and do what is right...

While Peter was still speaking these words, the Holy Spirit came on all who heard the message. The circumcised believers who had come with Peter were astonished that the gift of the Holy Spirit had been poured out even on Gentiles. For they heard them speaking in tongues and praising God.

Then Peter said, "Surely no one can stand in the way of their being baptized with water. They have received the Holy Spirit just as we have." So he ordered that they be baptized in the name of Jesus Christ. Then they asked Peter to stay with them for a few days.

In the same way, the Holy Spirit's job to indwell *us* as mentors—to lead us and guide us into all truth, modeling diversity and equality so that we can encourage urban youth to tap the same eternal source and be led into all truth as well, and to in turn model diversity and equality.

Most of us, if we're honest, have perceptions of "the truth" based on how we were raised and what we've been taught. Jesus knew who Peter was before time began. Jesus, being God in the flesh, understood learning and the developmental process. Children learn how to "construct" their knowledge through active participation and inter-pretation of information within their culture. In his book *The Inter-pretation of Cultures*, Clifford Geertz states, "There is no such thing as a human nature independent of culture." The culture we're birthed into is used by God to show us something about his nature.

The monoculture focus of the Jews back in Jesus' day was in-tended to show in types and shadows the coming of the kingdom of God. The Jews and Gentiles were distinctly divided then. For Jews, the aspects of the streets, the building and arrangement of houses, the religious and political leaders, the manners and customs of the people, their habits, and—way above all—their family life was much different than those of any other culture. Their religion wasn't just a creed; it pervaded every relationship and dominated every phase of life. This picture of Jehovah being our everything is what Jesus un-derstood as a little boy.

Jesus was introduced to some of the same ideologies and preju-dices that Peter was; but the difference was that Jesus' heavenly Father was instructing Jesus. And what Jesus heard and learned formed the basis of what he built all truth upon and based all his decisions upon. The Jewish customs and traditions that Jesus learned as a child enabled him to model the nature of his Father's kingdom yet also use relevant cultural symbols to do so. In urban youth ministry—or in any ministry—we must know about and utilize the culture in which we're ministering...but we must never allow culture to supersede kingdom.

It Began in Nazareth

It's believed that a clan of the line of David, from the tribe of Ju-dah, returned from Babylon around 100 BC to establish the town of Nazareth. Jesus' secluded hometown was nestled in the southernmost area of the Lebanon Mountain Range. Nazareth belonged to the ter-ritory of Zebulun and was very close to the important trade routes of Palestine. These trade routes took place along the International Coastal Highway that connected Egypt and Mesopotamia. The position of the town may have been the reason for the Aramaic name for Nazareth, which means "watchtower," as it was located 1,200 feet above sea level. Therefore, the people in Nazareth would have been able to watch the passing caravans of numerous nationalities. And the Roman legions frequently used this road to travel to the Decapolis. However, since it was located in a basin of the hills, the city was somewhat isolated and secluded from nearby traffic. So as a boy, Jesus would have been able to see the international travelers, but he was still protected from their direct influence.

Nazareth is located 16 miles west of the Sea of Galilee and four miles south of what was then the cosmopolitan city of Sepphoris. A hike up one of the hills of the ridge of Nazareth would have brought into view Cana, the hills of Galilee, Mount Tabor, Moreh, and the hills of Carmel. For the people of Nazareth, every view would have reminded them of the stories of Deborah and Barak, Gideon, and Elijah and Elisha.

Nazareth is where Gabriel spoke to Mary; it's where Mary, Joseph, and baby Jesus returned after their flight into Egypt. On first glance, the latter might seem odd—after all, many Jews didn't think much of Nazareth. In fact before he met Jesus, the apostle Nathanael asked if anything good could come out of Nazareth (see John 1:45-47). Why the disrespect? Nazarenes were known for their bad morals, lack of religious piety, and crudeness in Galilean dialect.

In Mark 6:4, Jesus described the citizens of Nazareth as "his own relatives and...his own household." Nazareth was a small community, and Jesus would have been considered another family member to the people living in it. In Jesus' day the adults collectively watched out for the children and youth. There's nothing new under the sun—children are best raised by a community. In most urban communities today, there are pockets of neighborhoods where the community looks after one another.

My Aunt Catherine and Mamma White knew everything about the young people in their communities; they tried to make sure we were taken care of. Mamma White was from East Austin; she was a foster mother, so there were a number of kids in her home. It's common for many "mothers" in urban communities to have kids come by on their way to school and ask them, "Did you have breakfast today? No? Let me fix you a plate."

Jesus left Nazareth when he moved into his call of ministry at age 30. After his time of temptation in the desert, however, he returned to his hometown and announced that he was about to fulfill the Scripture's promise of the coming Messiah. Jesus' declaration didn't go over very well. The small size of the neighborhood helps shed some light on the people's reactions to Jesus' teachings in its synagogue (see Luke 4:16-30). Everyone present the day Jesus read from Isaiah 61:1-2 would have known Jesus personally. It may also be assumed that several of the people were related to Jesus through Mary. This helps us to understand the significance of the people's shocked response to Jesus' claims that Isaiah's prophecy was referring to him.

The reaction of these villagers must have been very traumatic for Jesus' mother, brothers, sisters, and the neighbors who were close to him. The people of the town became so upset with Jesus' claim to be the fulfillment of Isaiah's prophecy that they were filled with anger and dragged him to the edge of the ridge to throw him to his death (see Luke 4:28-30). The people of the community must have been torn between awe of Jesus' wisdom and teaching and confusion over their knowledge of him as a local youth. They were now witnessing the young adult Jesus filled with the "Spirit" and fulfilling his ministry purpose.

Later in Jesus' ministry, he returned to Nazareth with his disciples (see Matthew 13:54-58 and Mark 6:1-6). This time the villagers challenged him to perform miracles, which he chose not to do. But the real issue was that the people of Nazareth didn't believe it was possible that Jesus could fulfill the long-awaited promises of God to send a Messiah. They were too familiar with Jesus' earthly qualities to entertain the possibility of any divine qualities. Jesus "marveled because of their unbelief" (Mark 6:6, NKJV).

PROPHETS FROM THE 'HOOD

How often do we struggle to believe that the troubled youth living in our own communities can change and actually thrive? Do we sincerely believe these young people can become the very leaders of our communities, enabled because of their journeys toward understanding their peers' difficult choices? I hope so. Because that kind of growth can speak into the lives of other teenagers and adults in their communities, tempered by a firsthand awareness of the troubles these individuals face. Yet often these young people are asked to minister in *other* communities where the transformation of their lives is more acceptable and believable.

Don't forget: Jesus *didn't* return to Nazareth after the second rejection by his hometown community. No wonder we dare not risk similar reactions.

Culture and Context

Various aspects of human nature—feelings, kindness, refinement, education, and culture—are all significant when discussing humanity. All human beings, no matter their culture, are entitled by the design of God to experience feelings of kindness and to have opportunities to be refined, educated, and exposed to the many diverse cultures of the world. The significance of culture must be considered if we're going to understand our human bloodline. Let's take a closer look at culture as it relates to where we're born and what family we're born into.

It's common for most cultures to establish a system of beliefs and behaviors that's agreed appropriate and conducive to the benefit of the whole of that culture. For example, years ago I was a guest speaker at the Southern Baptist Convention's College Week. While I was walking through the hall, an older African-American woman greeted me—not with a verbal sound, but with a gentle head nod. In that simple expression there was an exchange of communication long known among a people group who, when they weren't allowed to speak or didn't want to make a scene, were able to share commonality and a consensus of loyalty and recognition. To acknowledge someone's presence is a powerful thing, and most cultures around the globe have ways of meeting and greeting and acknowledging.

In their book *Counseling the Culturally Different*, Derald Wing Sue and David Sue share how every culture is built on a foundation of beliefs. These beliefs shape the culture, which shapes the people. The culture influences numerous aspects of people's lives: The way they think, their approach to prob-

Jesus Experienced Classism and Racism

Born in a stable in Bethlehem and growing up as the son of a carpenter from Nazareth, Jesus and his family were poor. Jesus was poor all his life. As such he was very familiar with the class differences afoot in his day. During his periodic visits to the temple, Jesus also witnessed the growing Pharisaic movement and the infiltration of Roman politics into the appointment of the temple's high priest. He watched as money gained more influence in temple politics, and the court of the Gentiles was used as the high priest's personal marketplace. Jesus knew the occupying Romans weren't the only ones stealing from the have-nots in his neighborhood. Those who were supposed to be keepers of the law were just as guilty of deepening class divisions— to say nothing of the Jewish tax collectors. Yet Jesus broke bread with the Pharisees, and he saw potential in one of the hated tax collectors and brought him on board as a disciple—Matthew.

Furthermore, the issue of race was never far from the boiling point in Israel, whether it came in the form of Roman brutality against the Jews...or Jews shunning the "half-breed" Samaritans. But again, Jesus just said a word and a Roman Centurion's servant was healed—and you know how he felt about the Samaritans. Yes, Jesus experienced racism and classism first hand, but his responses to both were shocking, revolutionary, and ultimately healing. To make inroads in urban youth ministry, we cannot do less than follow Jesus' example in how we teach and train teenagers and how we deal with others on a day-to-day basis.

lem solving, how they raise their children, and how they view their spouses. Culture also affects how children view their parents; how people communicate and worship; and how they view others; their senses of humor, diet, values, standards of beauty, laws, and household policies.

Culture mostly consists of the things people have learned to do, believe, value, and enjoy in their history. Culture can represent the totality of ideals, beliefs, skills, tools, customs, and institutions into which each member of society is born. Sue and Sue often stress the positive aspects of being bicultural. They also note that such dual "citizenship" might cause problems for many minorities living in an environment with a dominant culture. (In this case it would also apply to serving in youth ministry.)

Culture is something that affects all of us. But more often than not in the evangelical world, when a person of color mentions *culture* in a meeting, it tends to stir emotions and, at times, confrontation.

WE MUST WORK TOGETHER

In the United States, local churches run most youth ministries; parachurch organizations run the rest. Many of these parachurch ministries serve minority populations. But the design and operational plans are usually governed, structured, and supervised by a majority "European" caucus.

Sometimes one or two strong leaders of color are hired and placed in a visible position of the hierarchical structure to give the appearance of a "culturally sensitive ministry." These persons are given a platform from which to share, and everyone is excited that there's new blood on board. They're invited to meetings—some formal, some informal (lunch or dinner)—to share "stories." And in these venues, each people group is learning to say "the right words" and make "the right connections." Each culture is attempting to learn what's considered appropriate.

Other parachurch ministries have an international outreach, impacting cultures all over the world. This is often seen as the strength of being a diverse ministry. I applaud international ministries that fulfill the kingdom mandate of reaching the world. However, there are other issues to consider when ministering in the diverse communities of the United States.

When desiring to fulfill the call to urban youth ministry we must ask ourselves a question:

As youth ministry leaders, are we willing to learn from one another and trust each other's ordained identities as living models in the communities we've been commissioned to serve?

The only way this can get done is if we believe we're on the same team and willing to fight the good fight of faith together. Let's learn something from a certain famous leader.

Alexander the Great was a young, powerful man who acquired much notoriety. To know Alexander personally and to be recognized by him was the highest honor that a military man could receive. On very special occasions, Alexander hosted ceremonies during which he summoned soldiers who were hard working and especially brave to join him on a giant platform and stand by his side. Alexander then ceremonially gave public recognition to these special soldiers who had fought so hard and gone the extra mile in battle. Before a large audience of adoring military men, Alexander placed his arm around each of these faithful fighters and publicly declared, "Let all the Empire know that Alexander is proud to be the brother of this soldier."

The Greek word for *brother (adelphos)* carried the idea of a "comrade" or "fellow soldier." So picture yourself linking arms with the other leaders in your community who share the same vision to reach the youth of the inner cities, and then look at Alexander's quote with a twist:

> We are of the same womb of humanity. We share similar feelings, struggles, and emotions in life—but we haven't been conquered by these things. Like me, you're still in the game and giving it your best shot. Therefore, I'm proud to be affiliated with people like you—we are brothers and sisters!

Paul told the church at Ephesus to put on the armor of God. So to the believers of whatever city you reside in—a city that presumably has young people who need to be ministered to—let's get fully armed together. Now that our identity on the team is clearly understood, let's get fully dressed for the game!

Fighting Our Common, Invisible Enemy

We're told to "be strong in the Lord and in the power of His might" (Ephesians 6:10, NKJV). This verse talks about the supernatural power that God has made available for our fight with unseen, demonic powers that war against the soul. The word for *strong* in this verse is taken from the Greek word *endunamoo*, which describes a power that fills believers with a massive dose of inward strength. It's like those commercials that show someone gulping down a power drink, and then he or she is able to endure intense competition. This *endunamoo* power is so strong that it can withstand any attack and successfully oppose any kind of force.

The word *power* in this verse comes from the Greek word *kratos*, and it describes power that's acted out. It's not merely intellectual power; rather, *kratos* is demonstrative, eruptive, tangible, and others can see it with their own eyes. A ministry (or person) with *kratos* is one that handles business when it means reaching kids of the city. Not a word needs uttering; the job just gets done. In fact, this is the same power that raised Christ Jesus from the dead. (See Ephesians 1:19-20.) How 'bout some of *that* power? This is the power that's working behind the scenes to energize us for serious combat and to overcome huge odds.

The power of God's might—this is the strongest stream of power known in the universe. People don't possess this kind of power unless God gives it to them. The word *might* is taken from the Greek word *ischuos*, and it's the picture of a very strong person; like a bodybuilder; one who is "able," who is "mighty," or with great muscular capabilities.

So now that we understand the background, contexts, and meanings of these words, let's read Ephesians 6:10 again using the additional information we just learned: "Be strong in the Lord and in the powerful, outwardly demonstrated ability that works in you as a result of God's great muscular ability." With this kind of power, you're ready to minister in the city and succeed in your confrontation with unseen, demonic spirits that wage war against the flesh and soul.

It's important to be fully armed with spiritual armor to fight this battle. Spiritual resistance requires spiritual assistance. It's called the *full armor* of God. The armor is necessary to fight against the Devil's schemes. And the Devil has numerous strategies of offensive attack— discouragement, frustration, confusion, and moral failure, to name a few.

Remember, when God was laying out the plan for your life and my life, the enemy had not yet fallen to the earth. (In other words, Lucifer heard about your purposed potential before the earth was formed.) The Devil and his cohorts have since set up land mines throughout your spiritual journey to distract, distort, and deceive you. The tricks or "wiles" of the Devil come generally on one road, and that's the road of our minds. For example, Satan will plant thoughts such as, *Oh, I can't do inner city work,* or *I'm not from the right culture.* Or you may even believe a deception of another tune—that *you're the rescuer!*

The word *wiles* in Greek is *methodos* (*mete* meaning "with" and *odos* meaning "road"). So where does this road lead? In 2 Corinthians 2:11 (NKJV) we find out a little more: "Lest Satan should take advantage of us; for we are not ignorant of his devices." This word *devices* is translated as *noemata* from *nous*—for "mind or intellect"—and it actually means to fill the human mind with confusion or to attack and victimize the mind. This is known today as playing "mind games" with someone.

I've experienced this in different ministry settings. When sitting in a room with a majority of males, mostly white, the enemy would toy with my head as comments were said in jest that weren't funny to me. Or when you're in the room or on a team as a figurehead, with no voice. People have designed all kinds of ways to keep you or your ministry silent, especially if it's going to empower a people group in a community.

We must be content with who God has called us to be—and be willing to empower and cheer on those whom God is raising up, even if it means that our season in a particular ministry is up. That's so difficult to accept for those who've stayed in one place for 25 and 30 years. My question to these long-term servants is, "Where are those in the community who've been raised up to do what you do in a multiplied fashion?" Jesus did ministry—poured into the lives of those 12 men—and then he left, trusting what he taught them and sending the Holy Spirit to confirm and demonstrate it. Do we trust that God still moves like that?

If so, then don't let the Devil play with your mind by filling your emotions and senses with illusions that control your thoughts and ultimately destroy you. Be careful of who you listen to. If you consistently hear negativity and fault-finding with no affirmation, grace, or a plan to change what may not be going well, then evaluate the source. If we're going to get anything accomplished in our inner cities, then we must stop fighting each other—and ourselves—by listening to our own negative and anxious inner thoughts and start speaking truth and encouragement to one another. We must tell our emotions—from the Word of God—what to believe.

The enemy seeks to penetrate our mental control centers in order to flood them with deception and falsehood and ultimately control them. Once this is accomplished, he can begin manipulating our bodies and emotions as well. This is when we begin fighting one another in the ministry, rather than partnering together for the greater good and advancement of the kingdom.

The way to fight against this attack is to be fully dressed in the armor or gear that God has given us to fight the good fight of faith. Remember, your fight is against those individuals whom the enemy will use to speak to you. (See Ephesians 6:12.) Many people don't even know the enemy is using them. Innocently, they speak out of their perception of a situation, but they're actually being set up by the enemy to be manipulated into thinking thoughts of defeat, discouragement, and frustration. The only way to deal with this kind of attack is to do what Paul admonished the believers in Ephesus to do in the fourth chapter of Ephesians:

> Until we all reach unity in the faith and in the knowledge of the Son of God and become mature, attaining to the whole measure of the fullness of Christ. Then we will no longer be infants, tossed back and forth by the waves, and blown here and there by every wind of teaching and

by the cunning and craftiness of people in their deceitful scheming. Instead, speaking the truth in love, we will in all things grow up into him who is the head, that is, Christ. (13-15)

We live in a world—and sometimes a church and ministry world—where people are coached to be deceptive for the sake of saving the company, or to be the "best" ministry that's reaching urban youth. No one wants to look bad, so everyone is trying to save his or her job or reputation. But Jesus told his urban-leaders-in-training, "If you try to save your life [i.e., reputation], you will lose it. But if you lose your life for my sake and the gospel, you will surely find it" (Matthew 16:25, author's *paraphrase*).

God desires that we learn to love enough to confront one another in love. I once heard this called "care fronting." Relationships are crucial for us to press on with the task of reaching inner city youth. When a relationship with fellow workers is lacking, it's very difficult to confront them in love. When you consistently see ministry partners struggling or not performing up to their potential, make time to meet with them and ask if they'd like to come and fellowship with you or another organization that's doing that particular thing well. We need to support one another. And we mustn't dismantle what God may be blessing just because we didn't think of it first. Do we love our brothers and sisters enough to walk this way?

Before the Ephesus believers could get fully dressed for spiritual battle, they were taught about speaking the truth in love, forgiveness, and unity. In war you must be able to trust your fellow soldier. Just like soldiers need to trust their commanding officer and each other, those of us who are called to minister in the city must trust our teammates as well.

So my question to you is this: *Who has God placed on your team?* Once the team members are identified and trust among the teammates has been established, then we can begin to see the kingdom of God advanced in the city.

DR. RENÉ'S PRESCRIPTION
for New Levels of Diversity and Unity

- Be confident that Scripture endorses the elimination of discrimination
- Always allow Jesus to inform your attitudes about diversity and equality
- Be aware that gaining support from their own communities/neighborhoods is often difficult for emerging leaders (it was for Jesus)
- We must work together—across racial, ethnic, and cultural lines
- Remember that our real enemy is unseen
- "Care fronting" those you love will pay dividends.

Rx

QUESTIONS FOR DISCUSSION

Before reading further, look at 1 Peter 2:9-10. What an awesome God we serve. God wants us to understand that once we've been born again (i.e., become a child of God), we're all one race of people, and one family with God as our father. The challenge to all of us is that when we come together as a spiritual family we must realize that we're individuals with different backgrounds economically, socially, and emotionally. Our external selves (e.g., our ethnicities) are just one of the aspects of who we are. We must learn not only to listen to the Lord's voice in prayer, but also we must learn how to listen to our spiritual family members in order to grow together.

Can we take joy in knowing that God freely chooses to manifest himself through hip-hop music, through classical pieces by Bach and Beethoven, through rock, and also through traditional gospel? Of course. In the same way, we can take joy in knowing that God's presence can be manifested in any life surrendered to Christ. Let's see what the Scriptures tell us about becoming one nation of people under God and indivisible.

1. How does John describe God's kingdom diversity (Revelation 7:9)?

2. The Bible tells us what it will be like in heaven; how does Jesus say it should be here on earth (Matthew 6:10)? How do we know that *being a child of God* through Christ is an equalizer (Galatians 3:26-28)?

3. How should we be praying for and taking social action in our communities?

4. We must be willing to work with those who've been long-time members of our communities even if we don't understand or agree with all of their concepts. If they're Christians, we must be willing to be reconciled— not "to be right." Read Ephesians 2:14-16 and write down and discuss what the verses speak to you.

5. Read 1 Corinthians 12:21 and ask yourself in what ways you need the ministries and churches in your community. Prayerfully ask God in what ways you need to serve alongside others in your community also called to serve youth.

CHAPTER NINE

DESIGNED FOR WORLD IMPACT
CREATED IN GOD'S IMAGE
TO CHANGE THE PLANET

The church community would say the Great Commission—when Jesus told the disciples to go out into the world and make disciples of every nation or *ethnos* (people group)—is right out of Matthew chapter 28. The disciples were to baptize them in the name of the Father, the Son, and the Holy Spirit; teach them to observe all the commandments that Jesus had shared with the disciples; and tell them that Jesus promised to be with them forever—and wherever—they went. But there's a little more to it that that.

The time of commissioning wasn't just for the disciples, but also for all who call upon Christ's name. And in the book of Acts, Luke tells us that before his ascension, Jesus shared with the disciples that once the Holy Spirit came upon them, they'd be empowered to be his witnesses first in Jerusalem, then in Judea, Samaria, and the outermost parts of the earth (Acts 1:8). Wow! This passage is so powerful. Jesus told those who'd received the Holy Spirit's commissioning power that they'd be enabled to testify first in Jerusalem, the heart of the Jewish traditions and the home of the temple (God's house); then in Judea, the place that represents the line of David; and then farther out in the marginal community of Samaria. Jesus knew that once the disciples had matured to the place of ministering to the people they considered unclean, they'd be ready to minister to the rest of the world.

Acts 1:8 also hints at much about the progressive maturing process of the Holy Spirit in each of our lives. Jesus knew the disciples wouldn't feel comfortable—on their own power—speaking about another kingdom to their family members and other Jewish leaders. Which is where the Holy Spirit's power comes in. Plus, Jesus had already reassured them, just as he reassures those of us called to urban ministry in a diverse world: "All authority in heaven and on earth has been given to me" (Matthew 28:18). Now we know Jesus doesn't merely mean that he has all power and authority. He's received all power and authority, and he *gives it to us.* (See Luke 9:1.) Jesus is saying that when we operate in his name, we also receive the delegated release of God's authority upon our lives, and that the *very same* authority and *very same* power that was given to Jesus in heaven and on earth is also released upon our lives. This is the enabling power and authority we need for wherever we've been assigned to minister on earth.

We have to come to grips with the Holy Spirit's power in our lives. Do we really believe in that power? Is that belief backed up by our words and actions as we step out in faith? Or do we merely acknowledge the Holy Spirit's existence? I sense we're probably held back by unbelief more than we realize. As believers in the urban youth ministry venue empowered by the Holy Spirit, we're like those kneeling before kings in medieval times who were tapped on both shoulders when they were knighted, in essence saying, "I'm placing the mantle of authority upon you, and my whole kingdom is backing you up." In fact, we've been sealed with the promise of the Holy Spirit (Ephesians 1:13)—just as though we're wearing a police officer's badge that gives us authority to stop a whole line of traffic. It's this power that can help us connect with kids, reshape the urban landscape, and create inroads to the marketplace.

Jesus told the disciples—and us—"I am ascending back to the Father, but the work has not been accomplished. I'm leaving you here to do it." When Jesus said, "It is finished," before he died, he was really saying that he'd done his part—but now you and I in urban ministry are called to finish the work that he started at Calvary. The ransom price has already been paid, so now we must follow through with the mission of bringing back those who've been held captive in a foreign land of oppression and bondage.

For the last 20 years, I've heard story after story about Christians not being equipped for urban ministry—or not being ready to add diversity into their ministries. I've noted previously that I believe the blueprint for urban ministry—or any ministry—comes straight out of the Scriptures. In Matthew 28, Jesus said we need to do three things:

1. *We need to see lives transformed by the power of the Holy Spirit.* It's God's desire to see people set free from affliction and oppression. God wants individuals to be free from the forces that are controlling their lives. Sometimes systems are designed to keep a people group oppressed and impoverished. But the control center is the mind! This is why it's not just enough to merely preach the salvation message to young people. There are other issues to address as well: For instance, there are a lot of angry kids out there—and they're angry for a lot of reasons. Maybe they can't read or write. Maybe their home life is terrible. Maybe they're shuttled from family member to family member while their mom or dad (or both) is dealing drugs. But Acts 10:38 says that Jesus came to heal all who are oppressed by the devil. Therefore we have to show these kids Christ's love and give him room to bring healing. We have to spend some extra time with them after school. Help them write that essay. Teach them how to relate to and encourage a mom who's depressed because she can't pay the bills. And pray with them and for them.

2. *Jesus left us with the mandate to train.* The transforming power of the Holy Spirit is to be accompanied by teaching and training. You

can't change a territory just by declaring, "We had 75 kids come to Christ at the Friday Night Jam." We must begin to train young people how to live out the Christian life in their daily worlds.

3. *Jesus commissions us to teach urban youth the written truth of God's Word and how it has something to say about everything pertaining to life and godliness.* (See 2 Peter 1:3.) The challenge for most of us is the fact that we want the quick-step manual to urban ministry, rather than taking time in the presence of God to pray and inquire what we're to do. We must begin by getting to know Jesus—and beyond simply knowing he's our savior. To get to know a person, you *spend time* with that person. And the more you learn about the person, the more familiar you are with what that person's heart and desires. Knowing what Jesus wants in the urban mission field comes from listening to his voice on a regular basis.

BECOMING INCARNATIONAL

I often find that urban youth ministry leaders equate incarnational ministry with simply hanging out with kids. This is true to a point. But for effective urban ministry to young people to happen, we need to take a purposeful, proactive approach—but we shouldn't force it, either. Our young people can understand how we connect with God simply because they're around us when we pray about daily-life issues and call on the Name of the Lord when someone is struggling. This doesn't have to be done in a flamboyant way, but through a simple pause and question: "Do you mind if I pray about that?" There's something powerful about having a burden and the compassion to move when the Spirit of God prompts you—and teenagers will notice our authenticity (or lack thereof) in those situations. So be careful. Let's not remain stuck in a place of wanting teenagers to like us and spend a lot of time and energy trying to prove our authentic relationship with them. What Jesus desires is that young people see our authentic relationship with *him.*

TAKING BACK TERRITORY

In the summers of the early '90s, I worked at Kids Across America, a Christian sports camp for inner-city youth. In the inaugural summer, I designed the camp's *Kaleo* program and watched God encourage, strengthen, and empower the youth workers who brought their kids to camp. Every morning I'd meet with the leaders for praise and worship and Bible study. And during every session, we sang a Ron Kenoly song, "We're Going Up to the High Places." (*Lift Him Up with Ron Kenoly*, Ingrity/Hosanna!/Epic/Sparrow, 1992). The youth leaders felt the words were appropriate for what was taking place in the heavenly realms on behalf of the youth of their communities. These words were sung as a form of intercessory praise:

> *Let's go up...*
> *to the high places...*
> *to tear the devil's*
> *Kingdom down*
>
> *We've got to be strong*
> *We've got to be bold...*
> *We're gonna reclaim*
> *Everything the devil stole...*

The youth leaders sang these words while thinking of their own cities and the youth who needed encounters with God. This song is about going into enemy territory where young people, families, and communities have been held captive. Our mission was to co-labor with the Spirit of God to begin to teach, train, and equip urban youth to drive out the enemy from their conscious minds. This is what's meant by "making a people ready."

An urban youth ministry movement is all about teaching, training, and equipping youth, families, and communities to take back territory in the urban landscape. I do believe that if the focus would change from merely getting youth a ticket to heaven to also equipping and sending youth into the marketplace, we'd witness incredibly positive results of ongoing ministry to urban youth. But for this to take place, there must be a touch of God's presence.

You Can't Google the Spirit

Again—I can't emphasize this enough—we have to invite the Holy Spirit into our businesses, homes, and daily lives. A great prayer is simply, "Holy Spirit, come and indwell this ministry setting and situation. I need your help today." Often this prayer isn't prayed because we live in a day and time in which we're used to "Google"-ing the answers to our problems. Thanks to the technology we discussed earlier in the book, ours is an abbreviated, high-volume, silicon world that eliminates the need for personal contact. So much so that many of us don't believe we have the time to consecrate (i.e., set apart) ourselves to touch the heart of God through intercessory prayer. Yet the Scriptures are filled with accounts of men and women of God (Moses, Jehoshaphat, Esther, Nehemiah, Daniel, Hannah) who persisted in prayer.

To succeed in urban youth ministry, we must do the same.

But why don't we? It makes sense to converse with God, the Creator of all things, if we're having difficulty navigating the ministry course he's set for us. Could it be that we believe intercessory prayer and fighting the powers of darkness through spiritual warfare only worked long ago or is only for "really spiritual" people? Well, I'm here to tell you that neither supposition is the case. Our prayer lives are our main streams of power and creativity—and the only means by which we'll take back territory for youth in the kingdom. Believe it.

The Spiritual Discipline of Waiting

Throughout his epistles, Paul uses three analogies to talk about spiritual disciplines—the army, agriculture, and athletics. In my book titled *The Love of the Game: The Great Commissioner's Draft,* I discuss how individuals involved in each of these disciplines must be in submission to a commanding officer, master gardener, or coach. It would benefit us to have this same type of discipline as we ready ourselves for urban youth ministry. You see, those who labor in all three endeavors must learn the discipline of waiting: Basic training and constant drills prepare soldiers for battle; a farmer toils most of the year on the crops... and then must wait until the fall for the harvest; athletes work out and practice constantly to prepare them for a few hours when they compete. In fact, Olympians labor for four years in preparation for sometimes just one event that lasts maybe a few minutes. Waiting. Working at what we've been instructed to do until it comes to pass.

And after we wait, we still may not get the answer we want. No wonder so many youth workers—in urban settings and not—crash and burn. We want the quick answer or quick solution so we can "make it happen" or solve the problem. But some have sown for years before they see a change—if at all. *We are never promised to see the fruit of our labor.* All we're promised is that it won't be in vain. How that plays out we may never know. But in the end, it's not our battle—it's God's battle. And only God knows how things will play out. In the meantime, what are you doing for *you* so you can endure the difficulties of urban youth ministry? How are you handling being in an oppressed neighborhood? Are you apprenticing with an older, wiser brother or sister who can come alongside you and encourage you?

SEEKING A BLUEPRINT

In our modern world, we're looking for the perfect blueprint of the ministry structure. Our ways of going about this are numerous: We have strategic-planning meetings, core group meetings, module-development meetings, and event-planning meetings, to name just a few. The 15 to 20 minutes that we set aside to pray usually come at the beginning of our sessions, and then we wrangle through our meetings for hours—drawing boxes, writing on sticky pads, bouncing ideas off one another, and sharing the latest business plan from the bestseller list. Every so often someone will chime in and say: "_____'s ministry has a great program—let's take a trip down there and 'shadow' someone for a day so we can implement what they're doing!"

A pastor friend of mine once told me something completely contrary to that: "We all need to grow in humility and get in the habit of asking God, *What is it that you'd have me to do in this situation?*" This question still rings in my ears daily—and at times moment-by-moment. And it most definitely influences how I approach a basic question connected to urban youth ministry: *How do we better prepare to minister or teach children of color in urban communities?*

Let's use the illustration of education and literacy. If we're going to talk about holistic ministry, we must talk about the reading levels of our youth. How can we expect them to engage in deep Bible study if they cannot read? Researchers and other educators have attempted to eradicate illiteracy, especially among school-age children. But despite their attempts, many African-American children all over this country still struggle academically. Innovative programs providing early intervention, such as Head Start, have improved the educational experiences of some African-American students; but others remain "at risk" in their poor, urban schools. Some teachers—usually white, middle-class females—develop creative methods to reach and teach their African-American students; but many are unprepared to effectively negotiate the multiple tasks and roles that are required of teachers who teach students who are culturally different from themselves. (Edwards et al., *Surmounting All Odds*)

Over the last decade, youth ministry has taken initial strides toward new programs designed to facilitate improvement. However, these programs may yield outcomes that are superficial and short-lived if they don't involve grassroots people and community leaders in the hard work of youth worker instruction and training—individuals who can become powerful change agents. Michael Fullan characterizes change agents as individuals with a personal vision—and capable of building this vision with colleagues—who view problems as learning opportunities and are committed to the moral purposes of productive educational change. A fundamental premise is that each and every youth worker must strive to be an effective change agent; youth workers and executive directors of ministry organizations must be willing to roll up their sleeves and participate in a process of change that can be difficult, complex, and uncharted.

In short, they should always be asking God, *What is it that you'd have me to do in this situation?*

LESSONS FROM NEHEMIAH

How do we do this? Scripturally, Nehemiah comes to mind. He was a man with a passionate vision. This didn't come about because he read the latest book on "serving the poor" or "urbanomics." His vision and passion were stirred as he heard about the conditions of his community, and then he received his God-ordained direction through prayer. Solomon said, "We humans keep brainstorming options and plans, but God's purpose prevails" (Proverbs 19:21, *The Message*).

So what was Nehemiah's background? He had a full-time job working in the courts of the king. God ordered Nehemiah's steps so that he ended up with the power and resources to aid in a vision for Jerusalem. Nehemiah didn't take the royal position with that in mind. He was being faithful in the place where God had positioned him. Then, at the opportune time, God allowed Nehemiah's ear to hear about the broken walls of the city.

As we take a closer look at Nehemiah, let's revisit the question my pastor friend asked God: *What is it that you'd have me do in this situation?* And let's add a second question: *How would you have me do it?* These simple prayers remind us that as believers we've given up the right to choose our sphere of service in ministry without consulting our Savior. When our life is adjusted to God in every detail, that's when God has the opportunity to work in us and through us for his ultimate purpose.

Whether we're concerned about the rebuilding of the walls of our soul or the walls of the community, I've learned there's no winning without warfare, and there's no opportunity without opposition. Paul tells us, "A huge door of opportunity for good work has opened up here. (There is also mushrooming opposition.)" (1 Corinthians 16:9, *The Message*).

But even when we have God's blessing to pursue our calling, that doesn't mean we don't have things to learn first. Things designed to prepare us for the task ahead. (We mustn't forgo that step.) And how was Nehemiah prepared for his task? He was working in the government of his day, not serving in the temple as a priest or chosen by God to be a prophet. He was in the marketplace. We're told he was in a high position in the king's palace—the cupbearer. This was a place of real influence in the court. In the same way, it's important for us to understand that urban youth ministry comes in many facets, from education, to health care, to family services, and so on. Not only has God placed ministry colleagues in those places, but he's also positioned solid believers in the marketplace to extend grace, favor, and expertise to those in traditional church and parachurch venues.

One day Nehemiah's brother and some of the other Jews returned from a visit to Jerusalem, and they reported what they'd witnessed. "They told me, 'The exile survivors who are left there in the province are in bad shape. Conditions are appalling. The wall of Jerusalem is still rubble; the city gates are still cinders'" (Nehemiah 1:3, *The Message*). This struck home to Nehemiah; he more than likely felt the pressure and burden of the message.

What I appreciate about Nehemiah's response is that he didn't hold a forum or symposium, nor did he start a new seminary course on urban studies. His first response was to weep and mourn, and then he went to the only One who could help the situation—his God and Creator:

> When I heard this, I sat down and wept. I mourned for days, fasting and praying before the God-of-Heaven. I said, "God, God-of-Heaven, the great and awesome God, loyal to his covenant and faithful to those who love him and obey his commands: Look at me, listen to me. Pay attention to this prayer of your servant that I'm praying day and night in intercession for your servants, the People of Israel, confessing the sins of the People of Israel. And I'm including myself, I and my ancestors, among those who have sinned against you." (Nehemiah 1:4-6, *The Message*)

Nehemiah's prayer was one of brokenness and confession. He took the time to *reflect* on the *ruins*; he was *remorseful* over the indifference of those in and around the city; he *repented*, including his among the sins of the people; and he asked God to *remember* his covenant toward God's people. Nehemiah was familiar with the Word of God and founded his prayer upon the covenant promises he'd read as a boy.

The question remains with us today: *Have we wept over the condition of our inner city and urban communities as Nehemiah did—even as Jesus did over Jerusalem?* At times it's easier to send missionaries and money to the remote parts of the world, yet right at our doorstep there are often tragic, desperate needs like the impoverished state of our communities' educational systems, child services, and health care.

Nehemiah's next step was his *response* to the condition. He took some responsibility for his community. The place of *responsibility* is often short-lived because we're moved in our emotions and immediately react instead of resting in God's timing and direction.

Further, Nehemiah could rest confidently in his response—as the psalmist tells us that God surrounds the righteous with a shield of favor (Psalm 5:12). This is a picture of God acting as a garrison about us. God would go before us, and God's glory would be our rear guard. Nehemiah's actions were not impetuous; he allowed God to work in him a burden and then move the heart of the king to grant Nehemiah favor.

After Nehemiah heard the news about the ruins in Jerusalem to the moment God opened a door for Nehemiah to take action probably wasn't a 24-hour period; it took time. (Again...waiting.) Sometimes God allows us to carry a burden for quite a while. I believe God does this to let us know that the burden is from him. This is the kind of burden that settles deep inside your soul and doesn't let up. And how do we come to get those kinds of burdens? Obviously it can only happen with God—but exposure to others' circumstances is a great starting place, too. Do we take the time to get to know the kid who never knew his dad? The girl from a home with no hot water or electricity?

We must trust that God prepares us throughout our lives for our next encounter with him. Each step of faithfulness prepares us for our next assignment. Our present circumstances are the tools that God most likely will use for what he desires to do later in and through our lives.

God Will Make a Way

When Nehemiah found out about the walls of Jerusalem, as far as we know, he mused upon the Word until it was burning in him, and then he spoke with his mouth (Psalm 39:3 gives a possible picture of what this looked like). After four months, God—who was already working things out—allowed the burden to give birth to conviction in Nehemiah's heart until it was intolerable. The initiative wasn't in Nehemiah's plans, but it all began with God.

And when King Artaxerxes asked Nehemiah why he looked so sad, Nehemiah—despite his fear—gave the king the straight scoop. No theatrics, no clever persuasion. Just the plain truth. So why do we feel the need to relate convincing stories and testimonies to people of influence? Do we fear we have nothing worth saying to them? Solomon gives us some perspective: "The king's heart *is* in the hand of the Lord, *like* the rivers of water; He turns it wherever He wishes" (Proverbs 21:1, NKJV, emphasis mine). God is able to work a miracle at any time, in any place, and in any way he chooses. In urban youth ministry, too often we get in the way of what God can do because we have our own timetables, our own assumptions about what we need to do.

We draw up the blueprint of how the ministry should operate, call together the people and have them pray over it, and then we get busy soliciting the funds to get it done. Our pride often interrupts the flow of what God may have orchestrated. And after nearly 30 years of this journey with Jesus, I'm learning that when we push open a door that God hasn't opened for us, we have to work twice as hard to keep it open.

Nehemiah did go to work on the walls of the city, and he even recruited the people of the community. But none of these things happened until *God granted him favor before the king*. We need to remember that it all starts and ends with what God allows. That should be a comfort to us. After all, Jesus tells us in Matthew 11:28-29 that his yoke is easy and his burden is light. He's reminding us to take our burdens before God in prayer. Because when God wants things to start happening in the urban youth landscape, God will make a way.

The *blueprint* of the Lord is forever written in heaven. His plan is perfect and will be perfected in our lives and communities. David tells us that a righteous man's steps are ordered of the Lord. Most of us know that part of the Scripture, but it goes on to say: "If he stumbles, he's not down for long; God has a grip on his hand (Psalm 37:23-24, *The Message*). At God's appointed time, Nehemiah went before the king and asked for what he needed. He knew the source of his request was not the king, but Yehovah Jireh, his God.

Alan Redpath, the late British evangelist and pastor, powerfully spoke of preparation for ministry in his book, *Victorious Christian Service*:

I believe the "show business" which is incorporated into so much Christian work today is causing the church to drift far from the conception of our Lord concerning discipleship. It seems to be instilled in us that we have to do something exceptional for God as a sort of token, as an example of courage and of sacrifice at which everybody will gaze, open-mouthed, and say, "What a wonderful man!" You do not need the grace of God for that. Human nature and human pride will take us through many a crisis in life, and make us do what seems to be the big thing in leaving our home and offering ourselves for Christian service. "My, what a man," says the world. That requires no grace; it appeals to the flesh. But I want to say to you from the depths of my heart that it needs all the grace of God to go through drudgery and poverty, to live an ignored existence as a saint, unnoticed by anybody. For if this commission is behind us in Christian work, remember, always we are sent out to be exceptional in ordinary things, among sometimes mean people, in frequently sordid surroundings. Only the man sent by the King of kings could take that, and only the man with a true burden will ever accept it.

So Now What?

What do we do with all we've heard? If God has indeed called you to urban ministry, then I want to encourage you to prayerfully consider these five things:

1. Have you *reflected* on the broken places in the community you feel called to?
2. Has your heart been *remorseful* over the broken places?
3. Have you *repented* on behalf of the people and situation?
4. Have you *remembered* in prayer God's covenant promises to restore the land?
5. What have you done in *response?*

"SAVAGE INEQUALITIES"

Being an African-American woman, for years I've been encouraged to be sure our children get a good education. It's been proven that a greater degree of learning happens when there are more personal experiences with a new concept: In other words, *I see it, I hear it, I understand it, and I implement it.* If urban youth ministries are serious about meeting grassroots needs, then they'll take a closer look at what Jonathan Kozol calls "savage inequalities." It means that for many children and teenagers in the inner city, there's so much in the way of students simply getting in the school's front door, much less the obstacles in the classroom. And nobody wants to work with these kids. Therefore there isn't a lot of learning going on. There are incredible inequalities in the system.

Several years ago I went to a Friday-night youth ministry event where urban and suburban youth ministries connected to the same organization attended. I noticed that in their literature, there were several leadership opportunities for the kids in the suburban setting that weren't available to the urban youth. So I pressed the leader of the organization about it. The response? "Those kids [i.e., from the urban youth ministry] aren't leaders." Hold on! Leadership is a *learned trait;* you train students to lead, you give them an opportunity to lead. That's a savage inequality. Urban youth may be impoverished, they may struggle, but we can't hold the belief that they're inherently unable to become anything they set their minds to. And it's up to us as their youth leaders to show them that truth—to live it out by dismantling every savage inequality we're able to dismantle. And getting even more practical, we also must see to it that people of our urban centers are learning how to read, write, and do functional mathematics.

WHEN WE'RE "STUCK"...

Often in the urban youth ministry world, we can become stuck. Things just don't seem to be working. Maybe we're at particular place in ministry we assumed would be great, but now we're not "feeling it." Maybe there's a lack of fulfillment—or we fear we may have missed out on something extraordinary that God had for us instead. Whatever the circumstance, there are often measurable reasons behind it:

1. The first potential trapping or stuck place is *ideological myth*—expectations, beliefs, and assumptions formed over time through personal and professional ministry experiences. Their gradual formation gives them a strangely durable quality. For instance, boards of directors, executive team members, and even some youth workers themselves often place responsibility for teenagers' "at risk" status on the youth themselves and their families. (Edwards et al., "Are We All on the Same Page?") Indeed, while gathering data from urban youth workers during my graduate studies, my interviews revealed the consistent belief that students were disadvantaged because they came from violent neighborhoods and "unstable" homes and arrived at school or youth group lacking basic literacy skills. These ideological myths were in contrast to the experiences of some small-church youth workers who'd been serving in the neighborhood for years—some had grown up there. These women and men were making significant progress in connecting with families and the community and advancing the youth to literacy development and positive social skills and self-esteem issues. However, the executive directors and other

youth workers within the same organization never tried to adopt the practices of other ministries or community individuals that had already proved effective.

Sometimes we rely too much on our personal preferences rather than on what we need to do or have to do. We see things based on our own filters. Once when I came onboard an organization that was 60 years old, there was a perception of urban ministry—and that was the only perception. "Because it's the way it always has been done." Or we throw money at it and say, "This is how we roll." But that might not be what's needed. The question is, *Are we willing to let go of our ideological myths?*

Through simple collaborative efforts with those in the community and doing effective work, we can eliminate some of the ideological myths. For example, 1 Corinthians 12:20 says we are one body but with many members. Look: You are not gifted to do everything. In urban youth ministry, that might mean, "Hey, let's do what we really do well, and then join forces with those who do other things well." The disciples used dragnets for fishing, but it required everybody coming together to get the best catch; and yet so many church and parachurch organizations stake out their own territories—and yet there's a *whole city to reach.*

2. The second area of being stuck in urban ministry is improperly using the Word of God. What do I mean by that? Rather than allowing God to work in us after consulting the Scriptures, sometimes we "learn" ministry based on what we learn in a couple of Bible studies—and then, "Okay, let's do it!" That's improperly using the Word of God. Things have to go a lot deeper than that to see progress in urban youth work. We have to let God come alive in the setting we're in. Better yet, are we willing to find out where God's already working and joining believers there?

3. The final place of being stuck is when there's a lack of shared vision. We must learn in the body of Christ—especially in urban youth ministry—that none of us are an island. We were created to thrive in community. It's my prayer that as we understand how Jesus called the disciples to walk in harmony that we, too, will move in a true spirit of unity and collaboration.

Becoming a unified front is where we'll be the most effective. If we're unable to do this, the consequences are grave. Instability and disunity will undermine educational efforts because fewer urban youth workers will be paying attention to this issue. That leaves urban adults and adolescents with a sense of resignation and defeat. Instead, we must be united in spirit and truth so that the education of and ministry to urban youth will someday produce a generation that can effectively determine what the moral and spiritual quality of the world must become.

So come—let us build together. We are living stones being built together in order to build God's kingdom.

DR. RENÉ'S PRESCRIPTION
for Worldwide Urban Youth Ministry Impact

- Come to grips with and accept the Holy Spirit's power in your life
- Become incarnational
- Take back territory
- Realize you may never see the fruits of your efforts this side of heaven—and that's okay
- Study (and imitate) Nehemiah's example
- Trust that God will make a way
- Endeavor to eliminate "savage inequalities"
- Learn to recognize what gets you "stuck"

QUESTIONS FOR DISCUSSION

Our task in relationship with one another is to help others discover a relationship with the Father and their position in the new covenant. We do this "one anothering" primarily through encouragement. The New Testament speaks of about 30 reciprocal commands that tell us how to treat each other. These commands include: *Admonish one another, encourage one another, bear one another's burdens, be hospitable toward one another, and teach one another.*

1. These instructions are aimed at building up our inner selves. Is your outreach focused more on behavior modification or spiritual orientation? How can you keep your ministry relationships focused on encouragement and inner growth?

2. We're called to *stimulate one another to love and good deeds* (Hebrews 10:19-25). This presupposes that we believe God has designed us to be able to love and practice that love. Can you see the potential in the youth and adults to whom you minister to live this out? If so, how can you encourage them in their development?

3. Obstacles can keep individuals from seizing opportunities freely given to them. These obstacles can include fears, misconceptions, habits, and strongholds. How can you help individuals you work with "work" through these obstacles?

4. Sometimes the simplest solution is the best solution. Individuals whose life situations appear very complex are often helped by simple answers. But sometimes we complicate God's simple answers in order to appear to be taking every problem more seriously. What issues are you dealing with that may appear complex but could have a very simple solution? How can your presence, concern, and encouragement minister to the situation?

BIBLIOGRAPHY

Adam Clarke's Commentary, Electronic Database. Copyright 1996 by Biblesoft, http://www.godrules.net/library/clarke/clarkepro22.htm

Banks, James A., and Cherry A. McGee Banks, eds. *Handbook of Research on Multicultural Education.* New York: Macmillan, 1995.

Billingsley, Andrew. *Climbing Jacob's Ladder: The Enduring Legacy of African-American Families.* (New York: Touchstone, 1994) 28.

Committee on the Prevention of Reading Difficulties in Young Children and The National Research Council. *Preventing Reading Difficulties in Young Children.* Catherine E. Snow, M. Susan Burns, and Peg Griffin, eds. Washington, DC: National Academy Press, 2000.

Edersheim, Alfred. *Sketches of Jewish Social Life: Updated Edition.* Peabody, MA: Hendrickson Publishers, 1997.

Edwards, P.A., J. C. Dandridge, and H. M. Pleasants. "Are We All on the Same Page?: Exploring Administrators' and Teachers' Conceptions of 'At-Riskness' in an Urban Elementary School." In T. Shanahan & F.R. Brown, eds., *48th Yearbook of the National Reading Conference: 1999.* (Chicago: National Reading Conference, 2000) 329-339.

Edwards, P. A., G. T. McMillon, and C. T. Bennett. "Mining the Fields of Teacher Education" in *Surmounting All Odds: Education, Opportunity, and Society in the New Millennium Vol. 2.* Carol Camp Yeakey, ed. (Greenwich, CT: Information Age Publishing, 2003) 389-409.

Everist, Norma Cook. *The Church as a Learning Community: A Comprehensive Guide to Christian Education.* Nashville, TN: Abingdon Press, 2002.

Fullan, Michael. *Change Forces: Probing the Depths of Educational Reform.* Levittown, PA: The Falmer Press, 1993.

Geertz, Clifford. *The Interpretation of Cultures.* (New York: Basic Books, 1973) 49.

Heschel, Abraham J. "The Spirit of Jewish Education." *Jewish Education 24*, no. 2 (Fall 1953): 19.

Jaspers, Karl. *Man in the Modern Age.* New York: Garden City Publishing, 1951.

Kozol, Jonathan. *Savage Inequalities: Children in America's Schools.* New York: Crown Publishers, 1991.

Mishna (Kidd. iv. 14) from Edersheim, Alfred. *Sketches of Jewish Social Life: Updated Edition.* (Peabody, MA: Hendrickson Publishers, 1997) 168.

Morris, Aldon D. *The Origins of the Civil Rights Movement: Black Communities Organizing for Change.* New York, NY: The Free Press, 1984.

Redpath, Alan. *Victorious Christian Service: Studies in the Book of Nehemiah.* (Westwood, NJ: Revell, 1958) 34.

Sousa, David A. *How the Brain Learns.* 3rd ed. Thousand Oaks, CA: Corwin Press, Inc., 2006.

Spiro, Melford E. *Culture and Human Nature.* rev. ed. Benjamin Killborne and L. L. Langness, eds. Piscataway, NJ: Transaction Publishers, 1994.

Spock, Benjamin, and Stephen J. Parker. *Dr. Spock's Baby and Child Care: A Handbook for Parents of Developing Children from Birth Through Adolescence.* 7th ed. New York: Pocket Books, 1998.

Sue, Derald Wing, and David Sue. *Counseling the Culturally Different: Theory and Practice.* 2nd ed. New York: John Wiley & Sons, Inc., 1990.

Tyms, James D. *The Black Church as a Nurturing Community.* St. Louis: Hodale Press, 1995.

Wirth, Louis. "Urbanism as a Way of Life." *American Journal of Sociology* 44 (1938): 1–14.

Witty, Rabbi Abraham B., and Rachel J. Witty. *Exploring Jewish Tradition: A Transliterated Guide to Everyday Practice and Observance.* New York: Doubleday, 2001.

Through the art of "storying," your students will experience God in a new way. This unique, dialogue-centered approach will spark imaginations and inspire your group to find themselves in God's amazing story.

Shaped by the Story
Helping Students Encounter God in a New Way
Michael Novelli
RETAIL $29.99
ISBN 978-0-310-27366-0

visit www.youthspecialties.com/store
or your local Christian bookstore

youth
specialties

From the time they're born, boys are given a "code" to live by: don't cry, don't play with dolls, don't be a wimp...you get the picture. For a middle school guy, it's tough enough to figure out what it means to just be yourself—let alone how to become a man. This eight-week, interactive study will help middle school guys discover what it really means to be a man.

Becoming a Young Man of God
An 8-Week Curriculum for Middle School Guys
Ken Rawson
RETAIL $14.99
ISBN 978-0-310-27878-8

Media and culture tell middle school girls how they should behave, dress, and think—and it's not always a becoming image. This eight-week study will help girls become more—the young women God has created them to be. With fun and engaging activities and discussions, you can help girls discover their true value so they can become young women of God.

Becoming a Young Woman of God
An 8-Week Curriculum for Middle School Girls
Jen Rawson
RETAIL $14.99
ISBN 978-0-310-27547-3

It's hard for a middle school guy to figure out what a "real man" is, and even harder to find out how he'll become a real man. Show them the ultimate example of a real man as you help them study the life of Christ. With fun, interactive activities and age-appropriate questions, they'll discover how they can become real men of God.

Living as a Young Man of God
An 8-Week Curriculum for Middle School Guys
Ken Rawson
RETAIL $12.99
ISBN 978-0-310-27879-5

Girls today have a hard enough time living life as young women. It's even harder to live as godly young women. In this eight-week study, middle school girls will learn how to live as God calls them. Using fun, interactive activities and engaging discussions, you'll help them live life as the women of God they are.

Living as a Young Woman of God
An 8-Week Curriculum for Middle School Girls
Jen Rawson
RETAIL $12.99
ISBN 978-0-310-27548-0

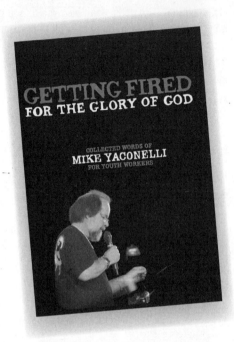

Years after his death, Christians across the world turn to the words of Mike Yaconelli to uncover the divine mischief, the shameless truth-telling, the love of kids, and the passion for Jesus that make youth ministry an irresistible calling.

Getting Fired for the Glory of God
Collected Words of Mike Yaconelli for Youth Workers
Mike Yaconelli
RETAIL $16.99
ISBN 978-0-310-28358-4

visit www.youthspecialties.com/store
or your local Christian bookstore

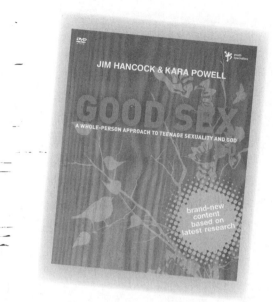

In this six-week study, you can help students deal with the thoughts and feelings they're experiencing after a divorce—whether it happened recently or when they were younger. With engaging stories and thought-provoking questions, students will explore issues of anger, guilt, forgiveness, family, and more through a biblical lens, offering them hope and healing.

Dealing with Divorce—Leader's Guide
Finding Direction When Your Parents Split Up
Elizabeth Oates
RETAIL $14.99
ISBN 978-0-310-27887-0

Dealing with Divorce—Participant's Guide
Finding Direction When Your Parents Split Up
Elizabeth Oates
RETAIL $9.99
ISBN 978-0-310-27886-3

BOOKS FOR STUDENTS

For students who want a new kind of devotional, *The Script* offers a new twist on the Gospel of John as they listen to and reflect on a spoken word translation from youth ministry veteran, and former rapper, Fred Lynch. Each reading is followed by creative exercises, as well as prayer and journaling to help students take the Word of God to heart.

The Script
A Hip-Hop Devotional through the Book of John
Fred D. Lynch III
RETAIL $16.99
ISBN 978-0-310-27806-1

Everyone has secrets, but you don't have to live with your pain all alone. *Secret Survivors* tells the compelling, true stories of people who have lived through painful secrets. As you read stories about rape, addiction, cutting, abuse, abortion, and more, you'll fi nd the strength to share your own story and start healing, and you may even discover how to help a friend in pain.

Secret Survivors
Real-Life Stories to Give You Hope for Healing
Jen Howver & Megan Hutchinson
RETAIL $12.99
ISBN 978-0-310-28322-5

Fun games, captivating messages, great small groups, and trained
leaders are only the tip of the iceberg when it comes to youth ministry.
Don't forget the most important part—your soul. Jeanne Stevens will
bring you near to God, inside yourself, into community, and toward the
future as you discover for yourself the answers to the deep longing in
your soul.

Soul School
Enrolling in a Soulful Lifestyle for Youth Ministry
Jeanne Stevens
RETAIL $15.99
ISBN 978-0-310-27496-4

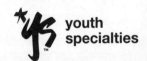

youth
specialties

visit www.youthspecialties.com/store
or your local Christian bookstore